THE WORLD OF JADE

OF

JADE

GREAT MASTERPIECES OF CHINESE ART

Text by Gildo Fossati

CRESCENT BOOKS
NEW YORK • AVENEL, NEW JERSEY

©1992 Yeh Bor-wen, Taipei
©1992 Fenice 2000 s.r.l., Milan, for the international edition
This 1994 edition published by Crescent Books,
distributed by Random House Value Publishing, Inc.,
40 Engelhard Avenue, Avenel, New Jersey 07001.

Translation by Jay Hyams
Typesetting by Christopher Hyams-Hart
Printed in Italy by Rotolito Lombarda s.p.a., Pioltello (Milan)

Random House
New York • Toronto • London • Sydney • Auckland

ISBN 0-517-10244-7
Printed in Italy

Page 1: *Flower vase in jadeite (height 8 in).*
Opposite frontispiece: *Statuette of celestial maiden
in jadeite (height 9 in). Both pieces are from the
Qing epoch. (See pages 96 and 107.)*

Contents

6   *Vase and chain in jadeite (height 7½ in).*

Preface

Li Po, the great Chinese poet who lived during the Tang epoch, the 8th century after Christ, and who died, according to legend, when he tried to grasp the reflection of the moon on a surface of water, was defined by another poet as being as "radiant as a jade tree standing in the wind." We associate the idea itself of jade with the Chinese, and long before it fascinated us that material had a certain fascination for them.

Since Neolithic times, that group of precious minerals that the Chinese collectively call *yu* (a word later taken metaphorically to mean anything that is pure and valuable) had been patiently worked and valued for its rarity. Translucent, as soft "as the morning dew," and wrapped in wonderful shadings of color from white to green to blue, jade was from the very beginning loaded with every kind of magical or mysterious quality and became an inexhaustible material for symbols: a tie between men and the gods, or the stone "of paradise," as it was also called. Believed to be indestructible, enormous amounts of it entered the tombs of kings to decorate and protect—a burial robe composed of more than two thousand jade blocks, sewn together with gold thread, covered the body of the royal prince Liu Sheng, a member of the Han dynasty, which ruled through several of the golden centuries of Chinese jade—and was shaped into forms of objects filled with ritual and religious values but also scepters, pendants, and jewels, profane symbols of prestige and authority. As jade was slowly freed from its function as a burial furnishing and was increasingly used as an ornament—of luxury and social prestige—for individuals and homes, the carving of jade reached amazing heights of refinement and complexity during the long period of the Qing dynasty, the Manchu dynasty, particularly during the rule of the emperor Qian Long. Minuscule objects were created and fantastic landscapes were sculpted on the surfaces of large pieces, rare blocks of green or white mineral. Pieces were created in imitation of ancient ones, following a profound characteristic of the millenary Chinese culture; the most refined art of jade was introduced in homes in the form of screens and jewels, small Buddhist statues, and brush stands and inkstands and paperweights on the tables of literati.

This world of jade has often been locked away in the jewel boxes of invaluable private collections, but an exciting window on it was opened in 1990 when one of the most complete and important jade collections—that accumulated over the course of twenty years by the passionate work of Mr. Yeh Bor-wen, of Formosa, and specifically dedicated to Qing jades—was opened to the public for the first time. Studied and arranged by the National Museum of Taipei, this collection of inestimable value has been the object of an exhibition in that city that is destined in time to visit other world capitals.

The ideal stop, enriched by pieces in addition to those included in the exhibition, is this book, which strives to give birth, filtered through the transparencies of the material and the evocation of its symbols, to an authentic and evocative image of Chinese culture.

Birds in jadeite: a parrot and two eagles.
(See pages 125 and 126.)

Jade in the Celestial Empire:

history and symbols

To say "jade" is to say China, yet the name *jade* is not of Chinese derivation but comes from the Spanish *piedra de ijada*, meaning "loin stone." The surprising aspect of this is that the reference to the loins—a result of the belief that the stone cured renal colic—actually precedes the Spanish definition, for the Romans called jade *lapis nephriticus*, "stone of nephrite," which is why the mineral (or, better, one of the principal minerals) that can be extracted from jade is called nephrite. Nephritis is an inflammation of the kidneys (which are the "loins" of the body), so as should be clear, even the Romans believed jade could cure kidney ailments. Thus the name of the stone itself reflects the fact that even in European tradition the beauty of this mineral's structure, its luminous reflections, and its transparencies, was matched by attributes of remarkable therapeutic qualities.

Jade appeared in China in the form of rings as early as the Neolithic period, in the 4th and 3rd millennia before Christ, during the phase of culture of the Long Shan and Yang Shao (Henan) dynasties. At Pan Shan, however, appeared the *pi*. The *pi* consists of a flat circle whose central opening has a diameter equal to two-thirds of the band. It is a symbol of the sky and is also the first symbol that appears in the complex Chinese symbology; it was soon followed by the symbol of the tiger, which precedes, in the order of symbols, the dragon. Jade was at first used only in the creation of symbolic objects. Its lucidity, the softness it reveals to the eyes, and the extraordinary range of its colors, from white to green to blue, conferred a sense of magic on the worked mineral. These magical values gave objects of jade a strong sense of mysterious powers capable of transforming the objects into symbols.

During the second millennium before Christ, in the Shang period, the number of objects made of jade multiplied: axes and knives as ritual instruments as well as the *pi*, tigers, and dragons. The tiger was a symbol of the west (and naturally autumn), the dragon the spring and the east. Later jade came to be used with other meanings, including as a representation of the emperor. During the Shang period jade was used for other purposes aside for those funereal, for in the tombs of that period are found not only objects made for use in the hereafter and thus imbued with ritual and magical values, but also daily objects, such as jewels, pendants, and buckles, objects which aside from being destined for the use of the dead in the afterlife must

certainly have belonged to them while they were alive. Beginning in this period, the tendency to apply the aesthetic qualities of the mineral to the production of pieces of clothing became increasingly common. The ancient use of jade was slowly changing. The availability of the mineral was limited, for jade was not to be found in the traditional Chinese area. Instead, Chinese jade came from Khotan, from the valleys of two rivers, the Karakash and the Yrungkash. During the period before the two Han dynasties (the Early Han and Late Han), jade was introduced to China by way of barter, the exchange of merchandise among the peoples of central Asia and China. Even so, during the Shang period and the successive Zhou period (1050-249 B.C.), the symbolic values of jade were higher than ever, and funeral furnishings were composed in large part of symbolic objects meant to accompany the dead to the afterlife. For this reason, numerous amulets in jade, representing various animals, such as the tiger, elephant, deer, buffalo, hare, rabbit, fish, turtle, birds of various kinds, and even the silkworm, appeared during the Zhou period. Another important symbol appeared at this time: the *cong*, a symbol of the earth in the form of an elongated prism perforated lengthwise and always carved of jade.

During the initial period of its appearance in China, jade came from the mineral called nephrite, which is a calcium magnesium iron silicate. Particularly luminous, it has transparent reflections. Jadeite, used for the production of most of the jade during the last two centuries of the Qing dynasty (18th and 19th centuries), of which we will speak later, is instead a sodium aluminum silicate that belongs to the pyroxene group of minerals; transparent and luminous, jadeite has a level of hardness on the Mohs' scale above that of nephrite.

Working jade involves an extremely difficult and laborious technique, for being a hard mineral, of the seventh grade of the Mohs' scale, it must be worked using an even harder mineral. The Chinese used sand as an abrasive, but the technique was an artisan's secret. To make the sand adhere it was kneaded with the fat of toads, and a kind of rotating disk seems to have been in use during the Shang epoch.

The Chinese believed that jade had therapeutic values, but their beliefs arose independently of any in the West; in fact, it is now thought that these beliefs became widespread in China long before they appeared 9 in the West. As we have seen, as early as the Roman epoch the Latin name used for jade indicated its curative powers over the kidneys, but well before the existence of Rome or at its earliest beginnings—in the 7th century B.C.—jade was thought in China to have properties that could preserve the body against decomposition. As a consequence, the first headdresses made to be placed on the dead were sewn and molded using jade inlays. This use increased, a few centuries later, both because of the increased availability of the precious mineral and because of the connection with the strong presence of Taoism, which during the 4th and 3rd centuries before Christ had worked out theories about the immortality of man and about the functions of jade in that area of belief.

The Han dynasty (202 B.C.-A.D. 9; A.D. 25-220) gave the greatest urge to the use of jade in art, and it was during that period that not only headdresses but entire suits of clothes were sewn in jade, using in these compositions small inlays held together by way of small holes cut in the edges of each inlay and then sewn together using gold, silver, or copper thread, according to the social standing of the deceased. This was in effect an attempt to achieve the immortality of the body, following the powerful Taoist concept that attributed to jade the ability of isolating the body from corruptive elements, thus preserving it from the process of decomposition. The tomb of the royal prince Liu Sheng of the Western Han (202 B.C.- A.D. 9), discovered in Mancheng (Hebei), contains a funeral dress made up of 2,498 jade tesserae joined by gold thread adding up to 1,100 grams. His wife, the princess Dou Wan, wore clothes made of 2,160 jade tesserae sewn together with 700 grams of gold thread. The coffin of Dou Wan was made of lacquer lined with 192 small jade tiles. On the outside surface, inlaid in the lacquer, were twenty-six jade pi. Evidently, that superprotected coffin was also meant to invoke the protection of the sky.

Jade knew the period of its greatest use during the Han period, which is to say until the first two decades of the 3rd century A.D. There was a historical reason for this. During the 2nd century before Christ, an emperor of that dynasty named Wu Di opened the so-called Silk Road, conquering and putting under the control of his troops those regions of Central Asia, including Khotan, in which were located the mines of jade—or, better, the deposits of that mineral. Thus, jade was no longer

something that had to be imported: for the first time, it was being produced on Chinese territory. With the fall of the Han dynasty (A.D. 220), these outlying territories were lost, and jade became rare again. For this reason, in A.D. 222, during the so-called period of the Three Kingdoms (3rd century after Christ), one of the Wei emperors, Wen Di, when he took the throne prohibited all the nobles and landowners from the use of jade in funeral garments. From then on such clothes disappeared from tombs, but not the belief in the rebirth of the body and not the faith in the abilities of jade to protect it. It was necessary, however, to reduce as much as possible the consumption of jade, and this was made possible by turning to the power of symbols. Use was made of the system of "plugging" the eight body orifices, including the eyes and the mouth. On the eyes were placed fish, symbol of wisdom and vigilance. A jade cicada was placed in the mouth, for according to Taoist theories the cicada was the greatest symbol of rebirth of all living beings since at a certain stage of its life it abandons the larva, the shell of the cicada, and takes on a new life. Thus also man abandons the body to move on to a new life. But the body that is abandoned must be integral. But there was yet another meaning here: the cicada (tiao) with its song activates the principle of yin, which is to say water, or rain; this is why, as Gieseler correctly explains, the cicada and dragon are often found together in the same tomb, for the dragon is the cosmic symbol of the sun and thus also yang. Thus the future of the dead, the life he or she was traveling to live, was assured to have the harmony of the seasons, since the warmth of the yang would not be separated from the rains brought on by yin. The jade would thus preserve the body.

During the distant Zhou period (11th century B.C.- 3rd century A.D.), in accordance with the beliefs in the powers of jade, before being buried the body of the emperor was fed with jade dust mixed with rice. According to the Taoists jade nourished the spirits. This is reminiscent of the period in Europe, many centuries later, when alchemists sought the elixir of life; but gold was the indispensable element for preparing their magic potions. In China, instead, jade was always the fundamental element in funerary furnishings for the well-to-do. Because of the magic of its powers it was the material best suited to assume those forms that, because of their mysterious meanings and their references to occult powers as expressed in symbols, were best suited for representing the forces of the afterlife and awakening the beneficial powers of which the defunct, in his or her temporary state of impotence, would have need.

Between the Han period and the Tang period (A.D. 3rd to 7th century), a fabulous being called the *pixie*, whose cosmic role was that of holding off any evil influences, appeared, carved in jade, in tombs.

The fact that Jade remained the most characteristic material of Chinese art is due in part to the fact that the difficulties of working it stimulated artisans to try out new techniques, thus obtaining increasingly refined works, more and more complex, more and more difficult to imitate. Thus, with the passage of time, jade lost its typical function as a material for funerary objects and became more or less an ornamental object, both for people and for homes. In this sense it should suffice to cite as examples the necklaces made for women of high society and the objects made for domestic use, the fruit of the most skillful application of secret techniques, such as the incredibly numerous loose balls, inserted one in the other, like the universe of planets.

Even so, the use of jade decreased in a marked manner during this period, evidently because of its high cost, a result of the fact that it was once again being imported from territory beyond China's borders. But a new impulse, or rather a development that had never been seen in the working of jade, occurred during the Manchurian dynasty of the Qing (1644-1912). Before this, during the period of the Song dynasty (960-1268), there had been a great production, refined and precious, of porcelain and celadon. Porcelain was a high-class product, but with styles and costs infinitely below those of jade. At court and among noble families, porcelain and celadon had in a large way taken the place of jade. Celadon, it should be emphasized, was a product created by Chinese potters as early as the period of the Tang dynasty (618-907), developed intentionally to imitate jade with its appearance of lucidity, its waxiness, its impression of softness transmitted to anyone who touches it. Like jade, celadon emanates a mysterious light, full of magic. Porcelain can be used to create objects destined both for tombs and for the domestic use of families. The working of jade thus became more than ever a product for the wealthy—exquisitely refined, but nonetheless elite.

During the succeeding Mongolian period (1268-1378) and in that of the Ming dynasty (1378-1644), due to a complex series of reasons and aesthetics, other materials were used while, of course, the production of porcelain was further refined, in the sense that new techniques came into play, new ways of decorating works, and new enamels. For this reason the Mongolian and Ming periods are more famous for the production of porcelain than for jade. When the Manchurian dynasty took the throne of China a new extension of the Chinese empire took place, beginning first with the acquisition of the Manchurian empire, brought as an inheritance by the conquerors of the throne of Peking. This was followed by the conquests of Kang Xi, who annexed Tibet, and Qian Long, under whom the Chinese territory extended, as during the Han period, toward the center of Asia and the south of China. Then deposits of jadeite were discovered in the region of Burma. From the Burma borders, by way of Yunnan, jadeite arrived in China.

It was like a rediscovery. Jade triumphed as it had during the Han period; but the tastes, techniques, styles, and culture of the Qing period were profoundly changed with respect to those of fifteen centuries earlier. Thus jade worked during the Qing period, and in particular during the reign of Qian Long (1736-96), reached new heights in terms of the quantity of objects produced and their variety as well as in terms of the beauty of the workmanship, a beauty that had never before been reached. Works were made with minuscule details, such as yard-long works on which were carved entire landscapes as detailed as those in paintings. It was enough to commit a single error, to chip one leaf or one arm of a figure, to ruin an otherwise flawless work. Screens, paintings, birds, vases, and a thousand other objects were made of jade, a gamut of jade carvings ranging from those of daily use to ornaments, from jewelry to items of pure artistic techniques, with artisans always seeking new effects and refinements.

Much of the jade used during this period came from Burma, but the diffusion of jade was also a result of the Qing dynasty's conquest of the territory of Xinjiang, which included the Hetian zone and its jade deposits, which could be brought to Peking without great expense. What happened was much like what had happened during the Han period, such that the quantity of jade available and the ease with which supplies could be had favored the use of that mineral and thus determined the rise of various workshops in which jade was worked and the development of a taste for jade jewelry. At court, in particular, jewelry made of jade and other minerals of which we will soon speak was in fashion. The jade from Burma, a tributary state, was soon joined by jade from other Chinese territory, after the conquest of the valley of the Jin River, once Burmese territory and site of deposits of jadeite.

The 18th century was truly a period of triumph in the working of jade in China, and that impulse continued throughout all the first half of the 19th. There was competition among the various workshops in the working of jade in fantastic and impeccable forms: the products of these workshops, destined in their time for the ruling class, have ended up enriching the private collections of half the world and constitute the showpieces of the Orient's major museums.

The Chinese word for jade is somewhat generic: *chen yu*. In reality, while *chen* means "true," *yu* means not only "jade" but also "pearl" and, in general, anything precious. Thus the name that Westerners translate as "jade" the Chinese take to mean sapphires or turquoise and so on. It can be assumed that this is why objects made of jade are always accompanied in both private collections and in museums by objects made of other precious stones. During the Qing period there was a large production of other precious stones, for they demanded the same work methods as jade: there were thus quartz crystals, jasper, amethysts, chalcedony as both carnelian and agate, topaz, lapis lazuli, and malachite. Also much valued was white jade, rarer than the green or blue forms. White jade owes its enormous value to the fact that the tiniest impurity is enough to depreciate it while, at the same time, it owes its enormous fame to the wondrous chromatic effects that skilled artists can create using those very marks and impurities. By the 18th century, works in jade made for funerary uses—those pieces so imbued with symbolic meanings—were only a distant memory: jade was used because it is beautiful and pleasing, and the skills of Chinese artisans, who always managed to give the best of themselves when faced with every difficulty, made up the rest. Ability and patience: years are often needed to work on a single precious stone. The jade workers of Peking, Suzhou, and Yangzhou became famous. These last created from a large block of sapphire, from Hetian,

in Xinjiang, a panorama of hills and woods with the representation of the hydraulic works of the mythical emperor Yu the Great, protector of water, who lived in the 3rd millennium before Christ. The work includes his portrait and, reproduced at the foot of this work, a poem written by the emperor Qian Long, incised in the stone with minuscule and yet extremely clear ideograms. This piece is in the *lou shou tang* ("hall of old glories") in the Forbidden City of Peking. Another work famous for its size—a piece of jade two yards high—is the portrait of the great Tang dynasty poet Bo Zhuyi, carved against a background of rocks with woods and pavilions. He is shown meeting nine old men. This time the sculpture is of jade from the area of Hetian. Another famous piece is the representation of a mountain landscape, with rocks, in autumn. The reference to the season is important, for one of the great qualities of Chinese artists is that of representing images, scenes, and landscapes tied to a certain atmospheric and thus seasonal environment. This stupendous creation was made in jade by the artisans of Yangzhou.

In the past and still today, jade's high value puts it out of the reach of everyone, and for this reason it has been imitated. Such imitations are made of stones that are softer and thus easier to work; they are also, of course, less expensive. Used to imitate jade are serpentine and steatite. Serpentine is a hydrous silicate of magnesium whose mineral hardness is varied, but it begins at a grade on the Mohs' scale lower than three. Its characteristics are translucence, waxiness, and a somewhat yellowish-green color, sometimes marked by whitish spots. Serpentine as a stone is somewhat economical and has the advantage of being available in various areas of China. It has been used most of all for statuettes and vases with handles of various rings and joints, which the workers, already expert in the working of jade, created with ease. The Byzantines made great and refined use of serpentine in their works of glyptics. The use of steatite was widespread in the Near East, and beginning in the 2nd millennium before Christ was used in Crete for making seals, one of which, from a later epoch and in a quadrangular form with the representation of the mythical Nessus, is today in the Cabinet des Médailles of Paris.

Much has been said here about the aesthetic power of jade, which wins out for its extraordinary beauty; thus its magical attributes take second place. This is, however, a mistake and, what is more, it goes against the spirit of Chinese culture, which holds on to old beliefs and the mysterious forces of old symbols represented in relief or incised in jade, for these symbols maintain and even increase their magical abilities. Thus, among the amulets incised in jade the ideographic motif of *shou* ("long life") appears frequently; and with the same criteria are carved the dragon that wavers among the clouds and the fish that plays in the water, for they involve the magic role of combating evil.

During the Qing dynasty the jade workshops were used to invent new motifs or to create pieces of special skill, all of which called for exceptional technical abilities on the part of the artisans. But not everything was expended in this battle of invention and skill; as so often happens in China during periods of great production of some material that has suddenly become fashionable, the artisans made use of motifs from the past, turning their eyes most of all to antiquity, when skill, imagination, creativity, and mystical sensibilities played a fundamental role, leading to creations full of fascination. Thus also during the Qing period the artists turned to the imitation of antique forms, those of the Shang, in bronze, those, also in bronze, of the later Zhou period. Taken all together, the examples date from the 2nd to the 1st millennium B.C. This ancient-modern union, an invention accompanied by the reproduction of an object already part of the history of the art, taste, and tradition of Chinese culture, demonstrates the great artistic heritage left by the artisan workshops of the 18th and 19th centuries.

The Chinese achieved unequaled mastery in the working of semiprecious stones because the traditions of Chinese artisans date back to the Neolithic period, with a continuity over time and with connections among all the epochs that no other people can claim. The Chinese are the only people of the world who can be said to have thousands of years of experience behind them in every field of endeavor. This is not only experience but technical developments, refinements of taste, with increasing demands made by clients. To this reality must be added the influences that came to China from other countries, influences that have themselves been accumulated over time, like the sap of tradition. During the Qing period important influences reached China from the knowledge of the peoples living in the recently annexed provinces, such as the Moslems in Chinese Turkestan, themselves in turn tied to the experiences of the central Asian peoples. A new aspect concerning the influences of foreigners was the presence in China of Europeans, who came to China beginning with Marco Polo and the numerous merchants who visited during the Mongol period. Europeans returned several centuries later, not in the role of merchants but as men of knowledge, as evangelizers belonging to the Jesuit order. During the reign of Kang Xi many missionaries were in China, all of them given special permission to visit court because of the emperor's interest in their culture. The jealousy of other religious orders and the resulting diatribes forced Kang Xi (1661-1722) to throw all the missionaries out of China's national territory. Among the few Europeans who remained after the expulsion were men of science and art whom the emperor Qian Long loved to have at his court, making use of their labors and their wisdom. One of the most famous among these was Lang Shinin, a former Jesuit of Italian origin named Giuseppe Castiglione. His paintings, in a Western style, had an impact on the Chinese school of painting, and Lang Shinin himself learned from the Chinese school.

The story of Lang Shinin can be taken as an example of the intense cultural influences during the 18th century. The period of Qian Long was marked by great growth in the commercial relations with the West (it should suffice to mention the great activities of the East India companies, which dealt in porcelain specially ordered by European clients and in Chinese vases, often made to order in particular designs or with special ornamentation). In the midst of all these relationships, it is certain that the Chinese workshops of the engraving and sculpting of minerals came into contact with knowledge of European products, materials, and techniques. Such influences were developed during the Qian Long period but continued during later periods, particularly under the emperor Jia Qing (1796-1820) and in certain senses also under the emperor Dao Guang (1820-50). The 18th and 19th centuries constitute a period of great ferment, with China closed within its wealth and its isolation until it was overwhelmed and its most intimate beliefs were shaken by the tremendous experience of the Opium War, which ended both the impossible dream of a centuries-old sovereignty and the Chinese people's certainty of their own special qualities as a people who had always found themselves at the "center of the universe."

Small bottle and plate in jadeite of the 19th century
(height of the bottle 2¾ in; diameter of the plate 2¼ in).

Jade,

a name for many stones

The special qualities of jade have found their ideal match in the aesthetic judgments of the Chinese. But when speaking of jade it is always necessary to keep in mind that jade is a mineral with a variable appearance, without any standard color and, in fact, without any uniform characteristics. Jade, first of all, is extracted from two different minerals: one is nephrite, and the other is jadeite.

Nephrite, also known as "soft jade," is a mineral at the sixth grade of the Mohs' scale, and, following ancient Chinese tradition, it is taken to include white jade, sapphires, jasper, topaz, and many other semiprecious stones. The most common colors of nephrite are white, whitish-gray, green, dark green, yellow, and even black. It is a translucent, luminous, seemingly transparent stone. According to its color it is divided in various categories of precious stones: if white it is jade, if whitish-gray or white-blue, sapphire, green or dark green is jasper, yellow is topaz. Topaz is the rarest and thus the most precious.

Hetian, in Xinjiang, is the major center of production of nephrite. Nephrite is found in large blocks of the same color, so it is well suited to the creation of monochrome objects and those that have a precise identification. Aside from the locations in Xinjiang, important deposits of nephrite exist in New Zealand. All the jade worked in China during the period before the 18th century, beginning in the Neolithic period, was composed of nephrite.

Jadeite, also called "hard jade" in China, came into use during the Qing period, after China's annexation of an area on the border of Burma that included the valley of the Jing River, where there are mines of this mineral. Minerals came from Burma under truly advantageous conditions, since they were coming from a tributary state of China. The mineral had been discovered during the period between the end of the Song dynasty and the beginning of the Mongolian Yuan dynasty, but because of the enormous difficulties in obtaining it, since it came from deposits on high and inaccessible mountains, the extraction had been abandoned. It was taken up again on a large scale during the period of the Manchurian dynasty, in particular during the reign of Qian Long (1736-96). The colors of jadeite are white, green, white-green, white-purple, green-purple, green-red, and there are even pieces of three different colors. The most precious jadeite is green with blue shadings, for it has inimitable reflections. In general it presents a range of variations that go from the opaque, the waxy, to the most luminous translucent brilliance, so much so that it cannot be equaled—and thus cannot be imitated—by the jade from Pakistan or by serpentine. Because of these characteristics Burmese jade is also called imperial jade.

With the working of jade at the highest levels, creating objects of unmatchable beauty, the Chinese won well-merited fame worldwide, so much so that—as has already been pointed out—the name jade immediately calls to mind the name of China. Even so, the artisan workshops in which workers employed all the secrets of working semiprecious stones, such as jade, applied the same techniques and the same criteria of engraving and achieved the same levels of refinement and artistic imagination using other precious stones. The most widespread stones during the period under discussion, that of the Manchurian dynasty, were quartz crystals, jasper, amethyst, topaz, lapis lazuli, agate, cornelian, malachite, and turquoise.

Quartz crystals can be compared to the crystal obtained chemically with lead; but while the latter crystal is a type of glass worked in a special way, quartz crystal is extracted directly from rock and as such is a mineral with a hardness put at seven on the Mohs' scale. Because it is transparent and colorless it is not easy to use for the creation of objects of art, but that is what was done in China, while objects from this stone are extremely rare in Europe: a famous single example is the plate made by G. Bernardi during the 16th century and today part of the collection of the Museo degli Argenti in Florence, Italy. In ancient China this stone was called by a name meaning "water jade" because of its transparency, similar to water. Produced in various areas of China, from Suzhou to Huzhou, from Yuzhou to Wuzhou and Xinzhou, today it is used to make lenses for eyeglasses and dials for watches. During distant times it was used to make plates, vases, and other precious objects of daily use, whose beauty was not only in the transparency of the stone but in its brilliance, which refracts light. Rock crystal is also called "colorless quartz," but when it includes intense violet shadings, as does one certain variety of quartz, it becomes the precious stone called amethyst. The Chinese of the Qing period made rings, earrings, pendants, and other forms of jewelry of amethyst. Amethyst is also known as "violet sapphire" because of its strong color, which in the intense light of the sun becomes a reddish violet. It comes from Sri Lanka, Thailand, and, obviously, Burma. It is placed at seven on the Mohs' scale, just like jadeite.

Jasper, a variety of chalcedony, can be translucent to transparent but is more specifically white, gray, or blue; the presence of impurities or elements of extraneous minerals determines oxides of differing colorations, and each of these colorations corresponds to a specific kind of precious stone. Jasper is thus one of these stones, marked by a broad range of colors that runs from red to red-brown, from yellow to black, with an opaque surface. Spread in Asia Minor, from which it takes the Western name chalcedony (named after the ancient Greek city in Asia Minor), it, too, is a mineral that the Chinese ennobled and made use of far more than did the peoples of the West. It came late to China, and its great diffusion during the Qing dynasty was probably a result of the great demand for jewels and objects of art provoked by the intense working of jade. The hardness of jasper is intermediate between the two kinds of jade: six and one-half.

Agate belongs to the same mineral concretion of chalcedony, but agate is far more famous than jasper and much better known and appreciated. Agate has a characteristic rusty color that is accompanied by another characteristic, that of not having a compact color but having, instead, overlapping layers, with variations in color between one layer and another. Thus, while agate has been used in the West most of all for the creation of cameos, in which the variations in color from layer to layer are utilized to obtain effects of relief or depth, in China those same effects were used to create decorative motifs of great aesthetic value. Agate was used most of all to make necklaces and pendants; but also rings, cups, and naturally statuettes. Aside from its fundamental color, which characterizes it, agate also appears in different colors, such as red, green, black, blue, and even others. The color is always in concentric circles, with irregular and fanciful contours. And not just this: the differences between one type of agate and another are even more striking, for there are some that are as transparent and luminous as glass, others that are translucent like wax, and yet others that are opaque. Each of these characteristics corresponds to a name, and to list them would involve writing a geology text. From the earliest times, the agate used in China came from various places: the major ones were the areas of

deposits of nephrite, which is to say central Asia, most of all Xinjiang and Turkestan. But aside from these traditional areas, other sources were located in India, Persia, and Japan. It should be emphasized that this genre of mineral is reasonably widespread and that even China has holdings, for which reason its employment and diffusion have always occupied a primary position.

Another stone used to make refined objects is topaz, an aluminum silicate mineral that includes fluorine and hydroxyl. Of a yellow or honey-yellow color, it is ranked at eight on the Mohs' scale of hardness. It is one of the hardest and thus most difficult to work of the semi-precious stones, and this is why its use began somewhat late, both in China and in Europe, where it was appreciated beginning from the first half of the 1700s. It often appears as a whitish or milky crystal, but can also be found colorless and transparent, with veins of honey-yellow color. Topaz is not found on Chinese territory; it comes from Burma and from the island of Sri Lanka.

Carnelian, also called cornelian, is another mineral from the concretion of chalcedony, like jasper and agate, and thus represents a variety of quartz. Carnelian is red, transparent, and translucent. Deposits of it are found in Asia in India. Like most of the other stones dug out of deposits of chalcedony, carnelian is used, aside for making settings for rings, for necklaces and other forms of jewelry, as well as the handles for goldwork.

Lapis lazuli gets its name from the Latin words *lapis lazulus*, in which *lapis* means "stone," and *lazulus* means "blue." Lapis lazuli is thus a blue stone, but in reality the color of this mineral ranges from an intense blue to a clear blue. This same mineral was called by another celebrated name by the ancient Romans: sapphire. Only during a later period was the name sapphire used to indicate a variety of corundum with an intense transparent blue color. In ancient China lapis lazuli was used for settings in particularly valuable funerary jewelry. The mineral cannot be found in China and has always been imported, the sources being the regions of central Asia—today's Afghanistan—areas of ancient Russia (Siberia), Pakistan, and Burma, with the best-quality stones always coming from Afghanistan. From antiquity without interruption, and thus also during the Qing period, lapis lazuli has been used for settings, for its beauty, and for the luminous force of its intense blue, which brightens the shining twists of necklaces, heavy with gold and precious stones. Among the

16

semiopaque ornamental materials it is one of those with the greatest value, equal in beauty to turquoise and good-quality jade. Aside from its use in settings, the Chinese have employed lapis lazuli to create statuettes, vases, and other small-size artistic objects. European jewelers have used lapis lazuli in the creation of similar works, but with less mastery than that demonstrated by the Chinese.

Turquoise can sometimes be used in place of lapis lazuli because of the similarity between the two stones. In fact, the chromatic tonalities of turquoise tend toward blue, with more or less marked shadings, along with clear blue. There are also varieties with greenish shadings. When the color is compact it can appear even like porcelain with its milky reflections; but it sometimes happens that the body of the stone has black veins, thin and very uneven. Turquoise is a hydrous phosphate of aluminum and copper, and its hardness varies, for which reason it ranges among the grades of four, four and one-half, and five and one-half to six on the Mohs' scale. There are even examples of lower grades, but these are obviously of scarce quality.

From earliest times, the most valued turquoise minerals have come from Iran. They reached China from Iran by way of Turkestan, for which reason the stone was also known in China as "Turkish stone." Oddly enough, this name came into being in a completely autonomous way, with no connection to the European name for this stone. But in Europe, the term *turquoise* comes from the fact that the stone reached Europe from Iran by way of Asia Minor and thus passed Turkey, so it was given a name that indicated Turkey as its commercial source. From this comes the curious etymological parallel: "Turkish stone" in China and *turquoise*, meaning "stone from Turkey," in Europe.

Like lapis lazuli, turquoise is worked in small sizes, and when it is thin, its nature as an opaque stone gives it a milky luminosity that makes it appear similar to porcelain. The most highly esteemed turquoise is of a clear, sky-blue color without veining. Unfortunately, it is the easiest stone to imitate with fake stones or glassy industrial products that have been well colored. In the imperial palace in Peking are several famous examples

of turquoise, including a scepter (*ruyi*) with nine small handles, a somewhat unusual form but of wonderful craftsmanship. The Chinese have used turquoise from the earliest times, and objects made of this material have been found that date back to the Neolithic period. As with lapis lazuli, its use tends mostly to settings, but it has also been employed in the creation of necklaces in a wide range of sizes, with rounded or irregular stones, like randomly cut prisms but with the corners softly rounded. Another use was as settings for rings. During the Qing period turquoise became one of the most popular stones after jade.

Malachite is another stone that the Chinese have used with mastery, achieving extraordinary effects by using its characteristic structure. Malachite is not a particularly hard stone and may, indeed, be the softest of all those in consideration: it measures four on the Mohs' scale. Malachite is a carbonate of copper, and its most important deposits are in Chile, Russia, and Australia, but it can be found almost everywhere, although in small quantities. Malachite is the green basic carbonate of copper, and like all carbonates it is soft. In a sense it is strange: when found it already seems to be a decorative material, for added to its splendid green color is the fact that it is made up of striking stratifications of color that follow a circular movement animated fancifully by the mass from which it is cut. The slices of the mineral have such a variety of colored lines that they are themselves a decorative motif. Working pieces of a material with these characteristics the Chinese made use of those lines to obtain objects, small sculptures, containers with lids, and so on, in which the variations of the veins of brown or milky white, or the diverse tonalities of green, which run parallel to the infinite harmonious curves, play an essential role in the final aesthetics of the object. The golden age of malachite was during the Qing dynasty, not as jewelry, being more or less restricted to the making of necklaces in that sense, but in the creation of small sculptures of domestic use, knickknacks of the most refined taste. The value of an object made of malachite is based essentially on the quality of its craftsmanship.

Hindustani influences

A vast range of precious stones created during the second half of the 18th century are known commonly as Hindustan jades. In reality, Hindustan has only a secondary role in this name, but due to a series of circumstances it serves the role of being a prototype and represents the complex of foreign influences that had an important function in the evolution of taste in China.

With the conquest of Xinjiang by the emperor Qian Long, China extended its area of political-administrative control over part of central Asia, where there were mineral deposits from which jade could be extracted. This was indeed important, but still more important, perhaps, was the fact that being extended into central Asia China came into direct contact with peoples of different cultures, beliefs, languages, and writing. By way of this world, whose culture was tied to southern Asia, China created a bridge that neared it to the Mogul (or Mughal) empire of India. The northernmost region of the Mogul empire, the area nearest the extension of the Chinese into central Asia, was Hindustan. We know the Mogul empire's contribution to culture, art, and science. It was a world completely different from that of the Chinese, even in terms of the bases on which its civilization was built. One of the factors marking the differences between the two cultures was the fact that the Mogul empire was Islamic, strongly impregnated with Moslem doctrine and all that is derived from it in the field of the arts. For example, a fundamental aspect was the refusal to represent divinities and the use, instead, of richly decorative elements, representations of leaves, vines, garlands with fruit, all of this always presented in intense colors. Another characteristic is the use of compositions dense with representations of characters from legends or popular stories, woods, trees, leaves, pavilions, horses, grass, and flowers. Mogul miniatures are famous for their compositional grace, for the joyous colors, for their architectural fantasies, and for their powerful sense of the fabulous.

Following the Chinese expansion toward central Asia, this artistic world came into contact with the creativity and imagination of the artisans of Qian Long. The contact between these two worlds involved the intermediate area between them, the region of Asia located between these two civilizations that in these circumstances took on the role of being a bridge between them. Less powerful, less developed culturally, it was nonetheless rich with its own traditions, in large part nomadic, and its own concepts of life, its own particularities. As a consequence, the conquest of Xinjang meant much more than just a new kind of relationship and cultural enrichment with the population living in that area and had important cultural consequences.

The objects that took the name Hindustan jade in China were made up of pieces made for domestic use, usually destined for use in the preparation or eating of food: bowls, cups, plates, and spoons aside from boxes, vases, incense burners, and other pieces. These objects were usually made of white jade and sapphire, but in some cases they were made of topaz. The special character of these consisted in the fact that they were covered with decorations, and they often had settings of pearls or other precious stones. But aside from the inlaid stones, the objects were often decorated with inlaid gold or silver. The external surfaces were embossed in high or low relief with vertical lines converging at the center, with floral decorations, intersecting rings, or vines. Another aspect of these pieces is that not only the object in its essential function attracted attention due to the richness of its decorative motifs, but even the base and the handles of the objects were meticulously ornamented. Such pieces show the clear influence of the Mogul culture, of Kashmir and western Pakistan. Products from these localities, with their expressions of that taste and those cultures, reached China and could not help but influence the tastes and techniques of the Chinese products. It must be emphasized that the influences that thus penetrated China were of a wide range. First of all was their Islamic origin; in the second place was the pre-Islamic culture still existing in those areas; the third element was European influence, because in the encounters among civilizations there was also the importance of the contacts that the Indian Islamic world had with the Arab Islamic world and that the Arabs had with western Europe. The introduction into China of works by Mogul artisans, works influenced by the development of the Arabian-European culture, contributed to the creation of a new type of artisan work, a new style that joined in itself all these styles, from the traditional Chinese to those that reached China along the routes of central Asia. The reign of the emperor Qian Long has the historical merit of contributing to the enrichment of the already rich artistic tradition of China. With him, China reached, perhaps for the last time in the broad arc of its age-old history, the height of its political and cultural power.

BOX WITH COVER IN JADEITE

Diameter 4 ¼ in. This piece in green jadeite is circular in form and has very thin walls. The external surface of the body is finely decorated with three rows of lotus petals carved in positive; the internal surface bears the same decoration in negative. The same motif is repeated in two rows around the edge of the cover, at the center of which a peony flower is carved amid elegant foliage.

PAIR OF PLATES IN JASPER

Following pages (22-23): *Width 9 in. These two jasper plates were worked in the style of Hindustan. Very thin, they rest on four small feet and have handles with attached rings. The surfaces bear relief carvings of floral motifs.*

BOWL WITH HANDLE-CUP IN SAPPHIRE

Width 7 in. This piece in pale green stone is worked in the style of Hindustan. It has a wide mouth, a handle in the form of a cup on one side, and two small relief-carved flowers on the other. The body is decorated with stylized floral motifs.

CHRYSANTHEMUM-PETAL BOWL IN JASPER

Diameter 4¾ in. Seventy stylized chrysanthemum petals form the finely worked body of this bowl, which rests on a round base bearing the same floral motif.

TWO-HANDLED VASE
IN WHITE JADE

Height 9½ in; width 7 in. The body bears delicate carving with figures of phoenixes, flowers, and plant motifs. The handles are shaped like elephant heads, the trunks of which enclose rings. The colors of the figures vary from red to green with inlaid precious stones. This piece was used for birthday celebrations, and its base bears the inscription "made during the reign of Qian Long."

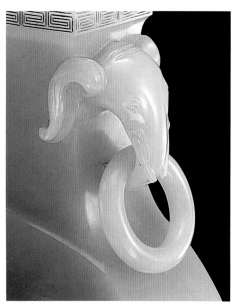

24

BOX IN SAPPHIRE

Width 3¼ in. This piece, shaped like a four-petaled flower, was made in the style of Hindustan. The cover is set with red and blue precious stones and bears flower and leaf decorations.

BOX IN THE FORM OF A DUCK IN WHITE JADE

Length 4 in. The cover is carved in relief to form the bird's head, feathers, and wings; it is inlaid with various precious stones, including agates. The half-open beak may be holding a piece of food. The figure's stylization contributes to making it an object of great formal elegance.

BASIN PITCHER IN WHITE JADE DECORATED IN GOLD

Diameter 4 in; height 3 in. This piece of excellent craftsmanship is in the style of Hindustan. The inner lip and body are inlaid with gold filaments and green and red porcelain to form the floral motif.

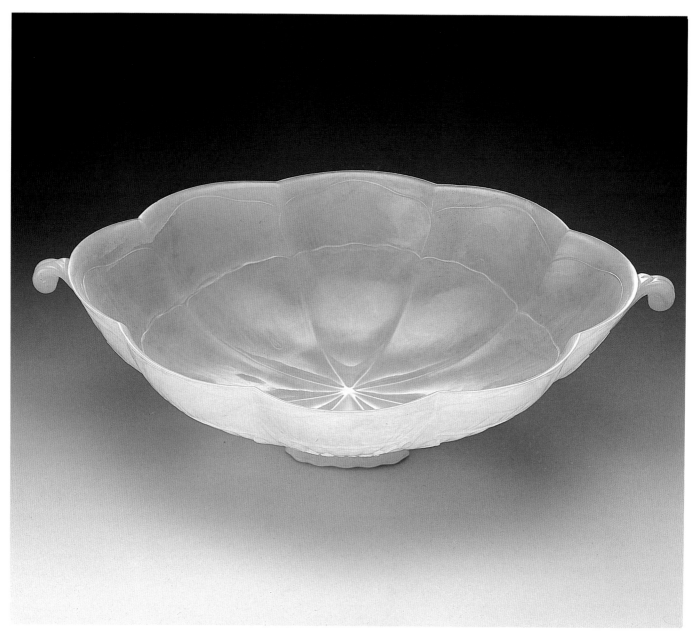

SHAPED BOWL IN WHITE JADE

Width 8½ in; height 2 in. The internal surface reproduces eight flower petals, while the external surface has a leaf motif. The base is in the shape of a four-petaled flower, and the small handles are in the form of tendrils.

HANDLED INCENSE BURNER IN JADEITE

Height 5½ in. The central body is carved with plant motifs inspired by the style of Hindustan and has two handles shaped like chrysanthemums that hold decorative rings. Four smaller handles that repeat the motif of the larger two decorate the cover, which ends in a flower-shaped knob. The base is also in a floral shape.

PAIR OF PLATES IN WHITE JADE

Preceding pages (30-31): Diameter 7 ½ in. The distribution of the pattern is typical of such pieces: the inner lip is elegantly carved with leaf and flower motifs, and the foliage theme is elaborated in the body of the plate. The skillful execution of these two pieces is remarkable given the extreme thinness of the material.

CHRYSANTHEMUM-PETAL PLATE

Diameter 6 in. The internal surface of the plate shown on this page is decorated with three rows of petals that spread outward from a round center in order to create the effect of a flower's corolla. The same motif, carved in positive, is repeated on the external surface; the style of the piece resembles Hindustani jades.

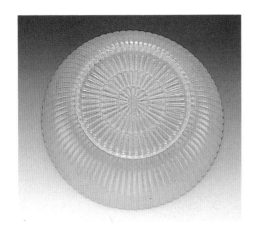

PLATE IN WHITE JADE

Diameter 6½ in. This plate of very thin jade is decorated with four rows of chrysanthemum petals carved around a small round center.

SHAPED PLATE IN WHITE JADE

Length 5 in; width 4½ in. The external surface of this plate is decorated with a background of chrysanthemum petals against which are carved in relief two peaches and two bats, symbols, respectively, of longevity and happiness. The extreme thinness of the stone adds further value to this plate.

LEAF CUP IN WHITE JADE

Width 4½ in. This object imitates the style of Hindustani jades; a flower and chrysanthemum leaves are carved on its internal surface. Elegant branches are carved on one side.

CUP WITH SPOUT IN AGATE

Length 3¾ in. This piece has a handle on one side and an undecorated spout on the other; the body is finely carved with thin vertical bands and rests on three small feet.

TEAPOT IN AGATE

Width 6 in; height 4½ in. This piece, decorated with elegant vertical carvings, has an undecorated spout and a handle in the shape of a ram's head embellished by a ring. The cover's knob is carved in the shape of a small flower.

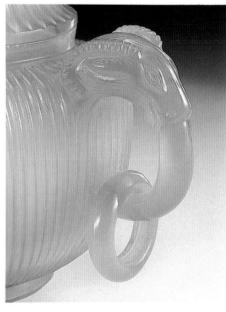

36   *Round table panels in jadeite (height 7 in).*

Functions and decorations in the home: the screen

The modern Chinese home has completely lost its original characteristics; most of all in city homes, the architecture is inspired by that of western Europe, even if the spaces allocated to each apartment are far more limited. In the countryside, in old houses, in the homes of the poor, one can still find traces of the traditional house. What is the difference between the traditional Chinese home and the type based on those of western Europe? The difference is that the European house—aside from being made of cement and not wood—is broken down in its interior: there is a bedroom separated from the kitchen. Even in the working-class quarters of large cities, where the apartments are very small and where many services are shared among many apartments, the fundamental subdivision between bedrooms and cooking spaces is common to all the apartments. The traditional Chinese home, as it remained up until the middle of this century, consisted of a single room used for both cooking and sleeping. Indeed, in the countryside during the winter months people slept right on the stove, called a *kang*, built in brick and with a large inward curve above to permit the body to find a position suitable for physical relaxation. Those who did not sleep on the *kang* slept on a table inserted in the wall, in a corner of the room, or on the ground on mats. Today the Chinese sleep in beds.

The traditional Chinese house was thus built for conducting a communal life, without the possibility of isolation. In China all of life is conceived as a collective participation, and this applies to *every* form of activity, from that of a worker, to whom apply the rules common to all the world's factories, to that of the peasant, to that of the artisan workshop: and even there work was done in a large community, with many rows of tables at which every artisan saw to the operations that had been assigned him. The product of such an artisan workshop is itself the result of group activity, in which each worker does his part at the appropriate phase of the work, giving the work his own specialized contribution.

Even though the home has changed with respect to tradition, the tendency toward communal life has remained one of the particular characteristics of the Chinese. Of course, one might well ask, if the home was traditionally built of a single room, how was it ever possible to separate oneself from the other members of the family in order to perform some function that required isolation, concentration, or solitude? There is a very simple answer to this question: the invention of the screen. The screen—which in its simplest version is made of a wooden frame with a number of upright poles covered with cloth—cuts off vision, isolating one corner of a room. During the Song period (960-1268), which has remained famous for the development of artistic-literary activities, the literati, that category of people who did not like working in public—in the noise, disorder, and movement of groups—adopted the use of artistic screens, with panels of jade inserted in a support of precious wood. Such screens were made of two parts, each worthy of the other. The panels made of jade could be round or quadrangular; they were usually carved in bas-relief with the representation of landscapes or plants, flowers, birds, as symbols of happiness and good luck; sometimes they were simply engraved with ideograms of popular stories, such as that of the "Eight Immortals." The wooden frame, of ebony or red wood, was made to hold the jade panels. Decorated with pierced decoration or bas-reliefs, the wooden portion of the screen was an artistic creation. In later periods the screen developed an alternative to wood with the use of lacquer. In truth, the supporting structures of the screens were still made of wood, but the wood no longer had to be precious, since it was made to be covered in black or red lacquer; and the decoration thus moved from the wood to the lacquer, in which there were usually inlays with the insertion of gold thread or with the sprinkling of gold dust in a changeable decorative context, according to the fashions of the times or the taste of the buyer. The two parts, that of jade and that of wood or lacquer, had to be in harmony, according to the Chinese artistic tradition. The screen was made of a changeable number of upright poles, from four to six and even twelve. The minimum of poles had to permit the screen to stand straight in order to carry out its role as a room divider. Both in the wood and in the lacquer can sometimes be found settings for precious stones. The screen, with the change in the structure of the Chinese home, has lost its functional reason for existing, but because of its beauty and decorative elegance, because of its intrinsic value, it has found a new reason for existing, no longer in the houses of well-to-do Chinese but in those of the West, where it works as an apparent separation while in truth it is only an object of furniture.

PAIR OF PANELS IN JASPER

Preceding pages (38-39) and these pages: *Height 10 in. The carving of these two panels shows great stylistic refinement. Depicted are landscapes with mountains, trees, ponds, and country houses, as can been seen in the details to the left and opposite, where illumination from behind brings out the shadings of color in the stone. The four ideograms in the inscription shown below give the period when the piece was made: "Made during the reign of Qian Long."*

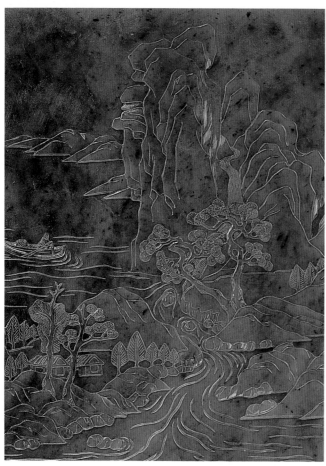

42

PANEL IN JADEITE

Height 8 in. The decoration of this thin rectangular sheet of green jade presents a mountain landscape with trees and a group of men unrolling a scroll on which stands out a "Tao" symbol (union of the elements yin and yang) in the presence of flute players (detail opposite).

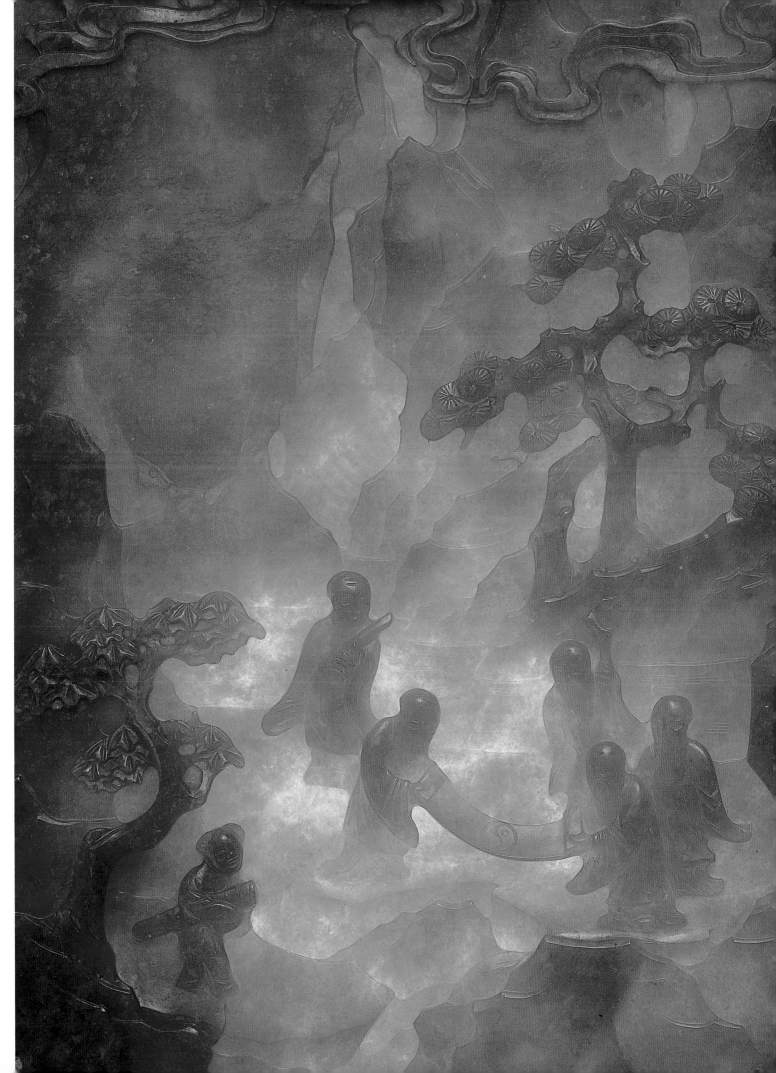

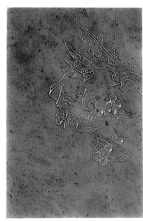

PANEL IN JASPER

Height 8 in. Birds, plum blossoms, and bamboo leaves are carved into this thin sheet of green jasper. The decoration is intended to symbolize the coming of spring. The panel was used as decoration in a study.

44

PAIR OF PANELS IN JADEITE

Height 7¼ in. Each of these pieces has a nearly oval form. The upper, circular part is decorated with pavilions and female figures on one side (above) and with phoenixes and peony flowers on the other (below and right). The panels are completed by an openwork base of carved cloud motifs.

45

PANEL IN WHITE JADE

Height 10 in. This panel, in jade of the highest quality, is carved on both sides with mountain landscapes and horses at pasture. The herd's young guardian appears on the back (opposite and detail at left).

PANEL IN WHITE JADE

Height 6 ½ in. The carving of this thin sheet of stone shows a scene of rocks against which stand out, amid flowers, mushrooms, and branches, the figures of a man with a woman carrying a duck. The back of the panel bears several inscriptions (left), including a black seal that gives the period when the panel was made: "Made during the reign of Qian Long."

48

PAIR OF PANELS
IN WHITE JADE

Width 9½ in. These panels are in the style of hanging scrolls with wide side margins; the engraved scene depicts figures crossing a classical landscape of cliffs and pine trees.

PANEL WITH SYMBOLIC
WISHES IN WHITE JADE

Height 6 ½ in. This rectangular slab is carved on both sides; on one side figures of the Immortals celebrate a birthday, on the other a deer runs across a landscape with trees. The object was a symbolic birthday gift.

PANEL IN WHITE JADE

*Width 9 in. The carving of this panel depicts a small
procession along a forest trail heading toward a large
palace (the pagoda-style roof can be seen in the
background): two elderly men are preceded by a man
bearing a standard.*

PANEL IN JASPER PAINTED IN GOLD

Height 9¾ in; width 13¼ in. This piece in dark green stone is elegantly decorated in gold on both sides. On one side is painted an elaborate landscape with pavilions, bridges, and pagodas across which various figures move; the other side is illustrated with trees, flowers, and phoenixes.

PAIR OF PANELS IN JADEITE

Height 17¾ in; width 14½ in. Each of these pieces in stone of variegated colors shows one of the mythic Eight Immortals: Han Chung Li on one panel, T'ieh Kuai Li on the other.

54

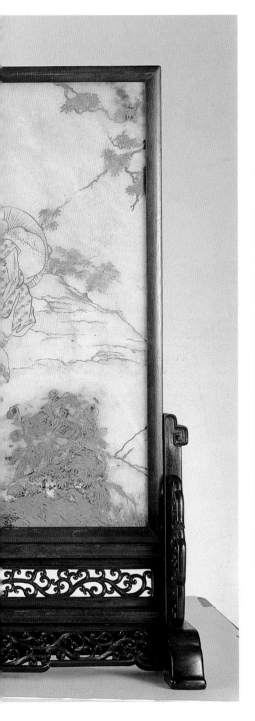

御製山村嘉蔭圖詩
重陰綠封覆弟堂邱堂遺
編共摧商董子鼎茶英好
緣相殿水乳正言長

PANEL IN LAPIS LAZULI

*Height 8½ in. Amid a landscape three human figures can
be seen through the windows of pavilions: two are
examining a painting, the third may be an artist at work.
At the top right is a gold inscription of a poetic work.*

**CARVED SCREEN SET
WITH PRECIOUS STONES**

*Height 48¾ in; width of each panel 9¼ in. This wooden
screen is elegantly decorated with carvings and settings of
stones that form motifs of birds, flowers, branches, vases,
statuettes, and brush holders. The inscriptions on the panels
date the work to the period of the Qing dynasty.*

58

SCREEN SET WITH
PRECIOUS STONES

Height 73 in; width of each panel 18½ in. This screen is composed of four wooden panels; the upper and lower bands of each are finely carved with a motif of clouds and dragons. The central band is set with precious stones arranged to form flowers, birds, and a deer with effects of great formal elegance.

59

SCREEN SET WITH JASPER

Height 72 in; width of each panel 16 in. These pages show the four panels that form this screen (the front is above, the back opposite). The upper and lower bands are decorated with openwork jade. The three sections that form the central part are set with jasper panels finely carved with flowers, birds, and landscapes.

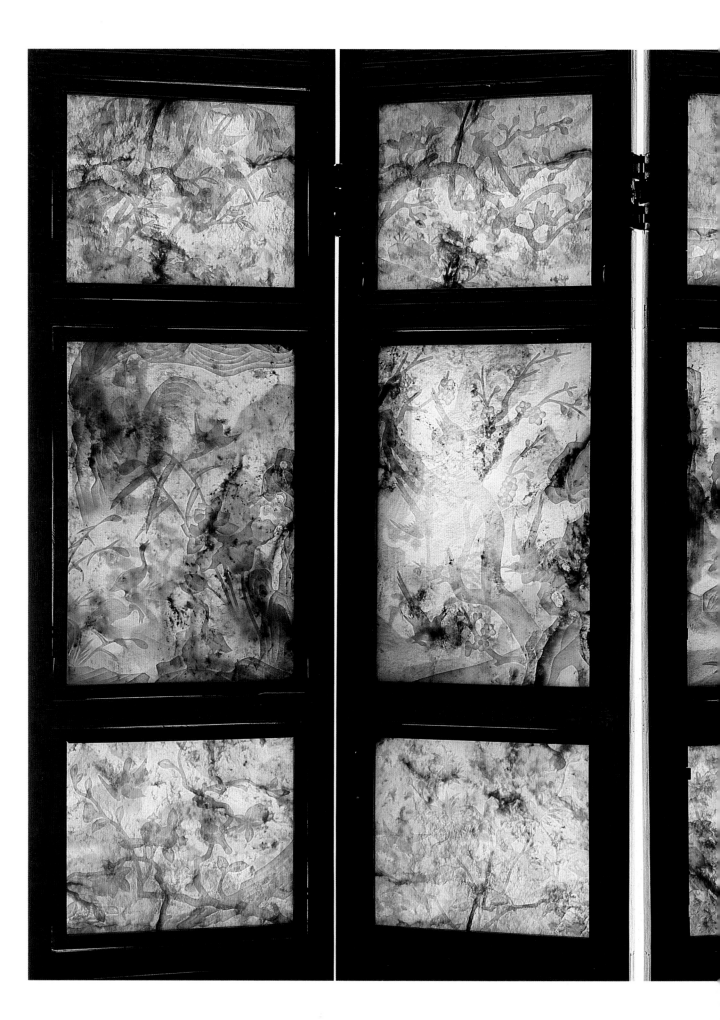

SCREEN SET WITH JASPER

Height 72 in; width of each panel 16 in. At left is the back of the central part of the screen shown on pages 60-61. Illumination from behind reveals the skill of the carving and the quality of the stone. Above is a detail of one section.

Jade like bronze:

the imitation of the ancients

During the ageless history of China, there was a period during which society was made up of a class of landowners who had a king and beneath them a mass of workers, artisans, and slaves. During this period, which occurred during the 2nd millennium B.C. and is known as the Shang period, from the name of the dynasty that then ruled China, the greatest symbol of wealth was the possession of a technologically advanced artisanal product: bronze.

Bronze is an alloy that appeared in Asia at the end of the 4th millennium B.C. The great discovery consisted in melting together a hard mineral, such as tin, and a soft and malleable mineral, such as copper. The fusion, done with the correct proportions, gave bronze, a hard, sonorous, and heavy material but with the characteristic of being moldable before setting and becoming hard. It has never been ascertained with certainty which people first adopted the technology of the lost-wax process. In China it appeared without doubt before the Shang period, but it was during that dynasty that it achieved its most refined manufacture, with the dignity of objects of art. These were not just objects of great value because of the fact that they were made of bronze, but their working, their fantasy, and the perfection of the execution of their forms gave these bronzes an unequaled value. A great abundance of bronzes from the Shang period have been found in diggings at the site of the ancient capitals, Anyang and Zhengzhou, both in Henan. The metallurgical artisans had the chore of creating utensils for use on sumptuous tables as well containers for use in the preparation and preservation of food. Thus was born the *lei*, which is the bronze version of the *ting*, the ancient clay pot used from prehistoric times and furnished with three long feet (tripod pots), between which wood could be placed for making a fire, since the stove had not yet been invented. There were also the *gu*, a chalice for use on the table to hold rice alcohol (the Chinese did not know wine until the reign of the Han dynasty, 202 B.C.-A.D. 220); the *jue*, another chalice, but this one made for sacrificial rites; the *ji*, a sort of glass, sometimes with a cover, with a large, squat form, which becomes a *hu* when it is slightly elongated in the upper part and thickened in the lower; the *yu*, another container for liquids with a cover and a handle; and the *fang yi*, almost a small sarcophagus in form, which was quadrangular with a pyramidal cover, made to hold cereals for ritual use.

It would not be possible to cite and describe here all the forms because the variety of bronze utensils used during the Shang epoch and later in the Zhou is incredibly large. The variety of the forms of these utensils is a clear demonstration of the rich imagination of the metallurgical artisans, who had to face all the difficulties of melting to obtain all the forms of these objects, forms that they either invented or based on still more ancient forms in terracotta, which they reworked to adapt them not only to the new material used but also to a new type of society, more refined and with a more well-to-do ruling class.

Another characteristic of these utensils was their external decoration, which wound around the objects like a band. These decorations did not serve only an aesthetic function; they had first of all propitiatory and magical functions. The animals presented were the dragon and the tiger or the snout of a strange monster, without chin or forehead, called *tao tie*: these were made to solicit benign spirits and drive off evil influences. Or they were decorated with clouds, lightning, and so on to attract to the fields the beneficent forces of nature. With time, these representations lost their original meaning and their symbolic value and remained as ornamental elements.

During the Qing period, the mark of wealth was no longer the possession of bronze objects but the possession of jade objects. We have seen how generic and all-inclusive the term *jade* was, used to embrace a vast range of precious stones. These objects were carved, not melted, like bronze: an even more difficult process. The artisans invented new forms for jade but also closely studied the forms of the past that had been used for bronzes, and they adopted many of these, both the shape of the containers and their decorations. Thus during the Qing period, in agreement with a standard practice in the history of Chinese art, artisans took as examples for their creations and for their work in jade the products in bronze of the Shang and Zhou periods. This practice had already been adopted during the Song and the Ming periods: but in the Ming, most of all, there was the attempt to reproduce the bronzes of the past with slavish imitations. The 18th and the 19th are the centuries of jade, not bronze. The imitations of bronze objects that we find carved in jade, in the infinite varieties of the past, always show fine workmanship, capable of exalting the new product, whose beauty reflects the taste of a refined, demanding, and elegant period.

SQUARE BRAZIER IN JADEITE

Height 10 in. This piece, made of pure, translucent jadeite, is an imitation of ancient Chinese bronzes. The decoration reproduces "tao-tie" motifs and clouds. Two lions form the knob of the cover (opposite).

BRAZIERS WITH DRAGON HANDLES

Preceding pages (66-67): Height 6½ in; width 9⅓ in. These pieces in pale jadeite streaked with green were made during the reign of the emperor Qian Long (Qing dynasty) in imitation of the bronze three-footed braziers of the Han dynasty. The handles are in the shape of dragons, and three figures of goats are carved on the covers. The central portion of the body is decorated with seven thin bands topped by a larger band in which the "thunder" pattern is carved.

HANDLED INCENSE HOLDER IN JADEITE

Height 8 in; width 9 in. This piece is made of jadeite with shadings that run from white to green. The knob of the cover bears two figures of lions, one larger than the other, that rest their paws on a sphere. The handles are in the shape of dragons and have decorative rings. Three feet form the base.

INCENSE HOLDER IN WHITE JADE

Height 8 in; width 7 in. The body and cover of this piece are without decoration. The knob of the cover is composed of two lions of different sizes. The handles are in the form of fantastic beasts and are decorated with rings.

INCENSE BURNER IN YELLOW JADE

Height 6¼ in; diameter 5⅓ in. This piece is made in yellow stone in imitation of ancient Chinese models in bronze. The body and cover are decorated with elegant and fanciful lines that reproduce figures of stylized birds. The knob of the cover is carved in a floral motif with four small handles with rings, and the snout of an animal is carved in each of the three feet of the base.

BOX IN WHITE JADE

Diameter 2¾ in. The cover of this round piece is carved with fanciful and delicate decoration; its body is smooth. This box was used to hold small objects or ink cakes.

INCENSE HOLDER IN WHITE JADE

Height 8 in; width 7 in. The cover, undecorated like the body, is topped by a lion-figure knob. The handles enclosing rings at the sides of the body are shaped like dragon heads; the three feet of the base rest on a decorative support. The overall effect is of splendid elegance and perfect stability.

SQUARE INCENSE BURNER IN JADEITE

Opposite: Height 9 in. This object was carved from a single block of white stone with splendid formal results. A stylized lion appears atop the cover, and minuscule bosses carved in relief constitute the principal decorative motif.

INCENSE BURNER, ROUND BOX, AND VASE IN JASPER

Height of the incense burner 4 in; diameter of the box 2 in; height of the vase 5 in. These three pieces carved of dark green jasper were used as containers for ritual offerings to Buddha. The form and decoration of the box and vase imitate ancient Chinese bronzes; the "baroque" aspects of the incense burner date it without doubt to the period of Qian Long.

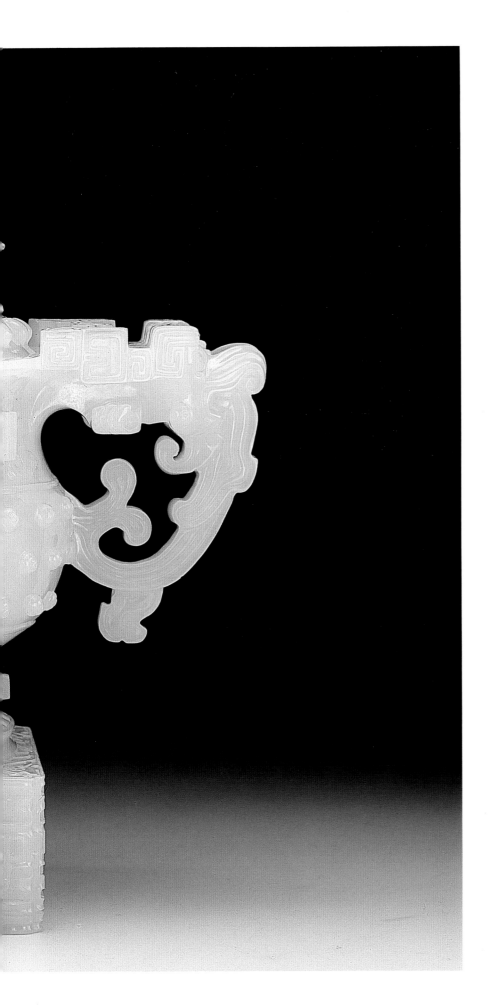

INCENSE BURNER IN WHITE JADE

Height 7 1/3 in. This piece was carved from a single block of pure white jade, translucent and clear. The knob of the cover is formed by two figures of goats carved in full relief. The handles are in a "baroque" style. The style is similar to the artistic taste of the reign of the emperor Qian Long (Qing dynasty).

INCENSE BURNER IN JASPER

Height 7 in. This piece follows the style of ancient Chinese bronzes. The handles of the knob bear rings, as do those of the handles on the body, which are in a plant motif. The carvings of the cover and body are reminiscent of the idea of the "tao-tie."

TEAPOT IN WHITE JADE AND SEAL IN JADEITE

Width of teapot 8 in; height of seal 3⅓ in. The central band of the body of the teapot is carved, and the spout and handle bear similar decorations and are embellished with rings. The handle of the seal has a zoomorphic form.

KETTLE IN JASPER

Opposite: Height 13 in. This piece was based on the model of ancient Chinese bronzes: the long handle, cover, and delicate and abstract decoration on the neck and central band of the body evoke the taste of earlier times.

PAIR OF OCTAGONAL LAMPS IN JASPER

Preceding pages (78-79) and these pages (details): *Height 17 in.
Each of these lamps is made of eight rectangular panels of
green jasper with relief carvings of flowers and birds. Even
the accessory parts that complete the lamps are finely worked
and bear inscriptions that indicate that the lamps were used
for palace illumination during the reign of Qian Long.*

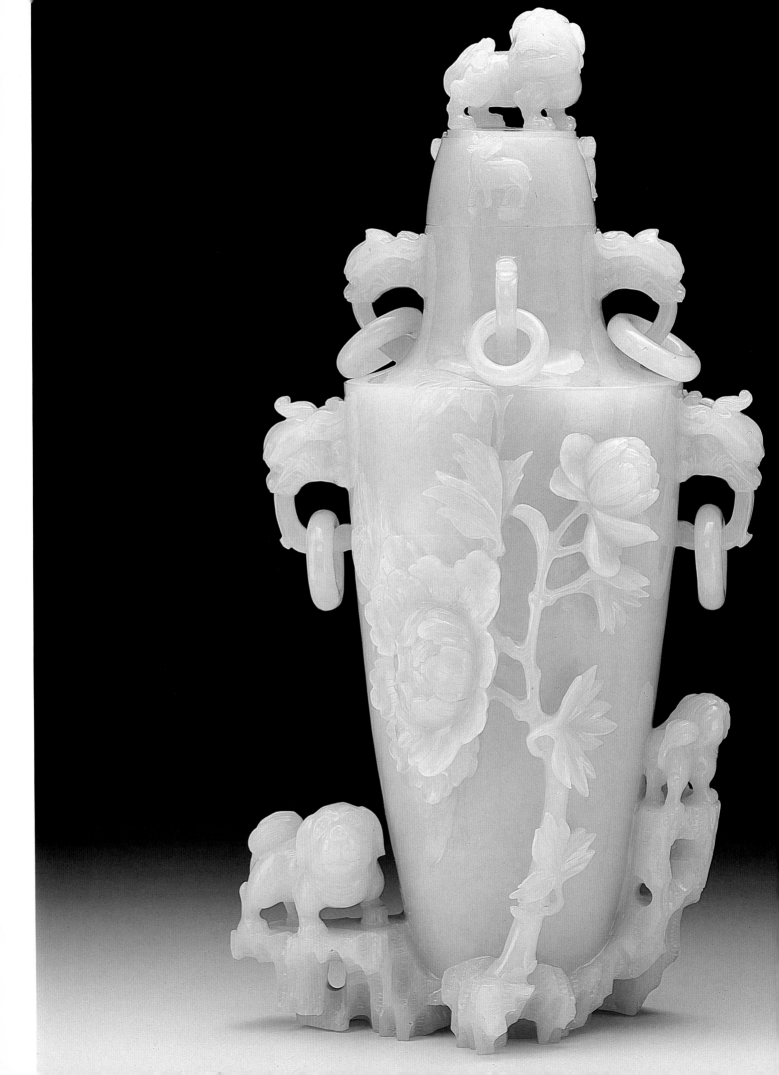

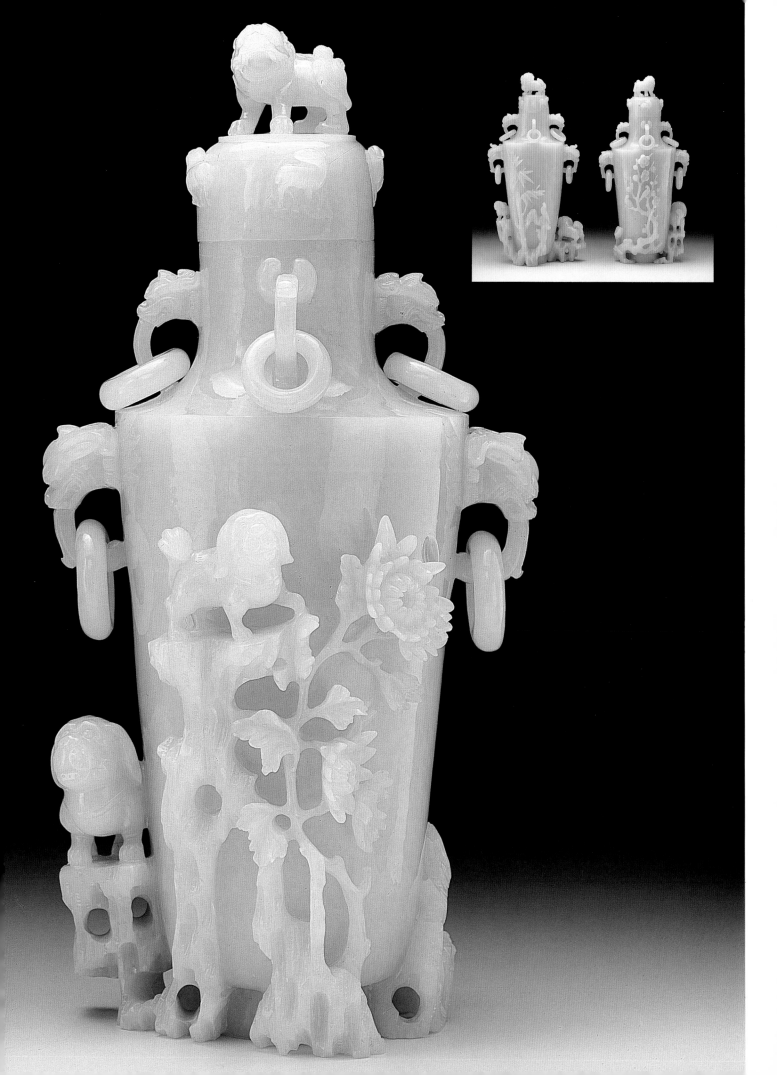

PAIR OF VASES IN WHITE JADE

Preceding pages (82-83): *Height 11 in. These pieces present particularly elaborate workmanship; figures of lions, one of which forms the knob of the cover, appear along with flowers. Six decorative handles with rings complete the decoration of these refined pieces.*

VASE IN ROCK CRYSTAL

Right: *Height 10 in. On the top of the cover of this vase is carved a Mandarin duck holding lotus flowers in its beak. The cover has four handles in the shape of animal heads with rings, and four more similar handles appear on the neck of the vase. The body is decorated with floral motifs.*

HANDLED VASES IN JADEITE

Opposite top: *Height 4 1/2 in. These two finely carved pieces are imitations of ancient Chinese bronzes, although they have a slight variation: each has three small handles with rings.*

INCENSE BURNER, BOX, AND VASE

Opposite bottom: *Height 1-3 in. These three pieces are in clear, shiny white jade. The forms follow those of ancient Chinese bronzes. The decorations on each piece are composed of abstract ornamental motifs.*

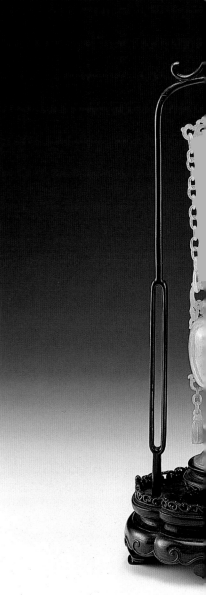

VASE WITH COVER AND CHAIN

Height 9¾ in. The white jade from which this piece was made has a special shine because of the stone's purity. The chain that joins the ring on the neck to the double ring that forms the handle of the cover is completely movable. The handles are decorated with floral motifs, and the surface and base are decorated with abstract lines.

KETTLE WITH HANDLE IN JADEITE

Height 11⅓ in. This piece is of white stone with blue streaks, translucent and semitransparent. The handle in the form of a chain is connected to the two handles that project from the neck. The knob of the cover is decorated with two rings. There are other rings near the bottom of the body from which pendants hang toward the elegant base.

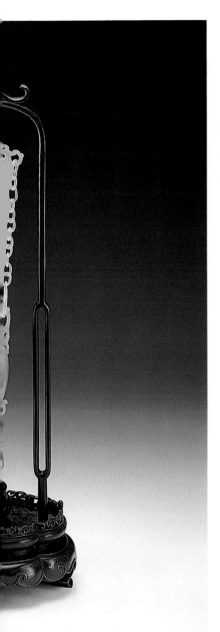

VASE WITH CHAIN IN JADEITE

Height 9 in. This piece is masterfully carved in the style of the middle period of the Qing dynasty. Figures of phoenixes are carved on the cover and around the base. A chain with only a few links is inserted in the handles projecting from the neck. 87

VASE WITH COVER IN JADEITE

Height 9 in. The jadeite used to make this piece has shadings that vary from dark green almost to white. The knob of the cover is decorated by a phoenix carved in full relief. The handles at the neck of the vase bear rings, and the body has figures in high relief: a pine, bird, squirrel. This piece was used for interior decoration.

VASE WITH DRAGON KNOB

Height 11 in. This piece is of great formal elegance. A dragon is carved on the cover, and around the neck are zoomorphic handles bearing rings. A "cord" of decoration runs around the base of the neck, and the upper and lower areas of the body are decorated with leaf patterns.

VASE IN WHITE JADE

Height 7 in. This piece shows the stylistic influence of central Asia. The main handle has an ornamental motif of branches, flowers, and leaves, and a ring hangs from the smaller handle on the opposite side. The body of the vase is divided in three strips decorated with abstract motifs.

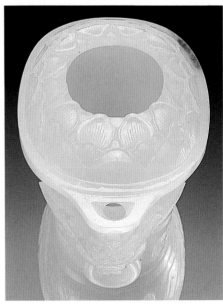

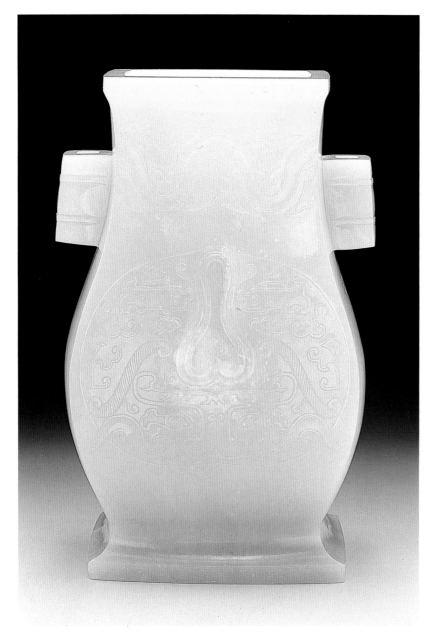

VASE IN SAPPHIRE

Height 9⅓ in. This piece is made of sapphire of the highest quality. Its form is taken from ancient Chinese square bronze vases. The decorations carved into the surface are fanciful but symmetrical, and in the lower part they are somewhat reminiscent of the "tao-tie" motif. At the sides are handles.

SQUARE VASE IN TOPAZ

Height 6 in. The topaz from which this piece was made is of the best and rarest quality. The form imitates that of a type of ancient Chinese bronze vase. The surface is smooth, but the handles are carved in the form of hornless dragons.

PAIR OF VASES IN JADEITE

Height 7 in. These two square pieces were made from stone of variously shaded colors. The four faces alternately present flowering branches and branches of bamboo. These vases were used both for practical purposes and as interior decorations.

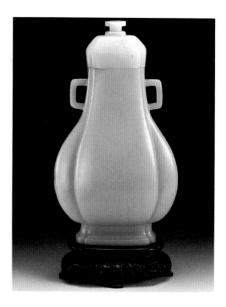

HANDLED VASE IN JADE

Height 9¾ in; width 5½ in. This piece in white jade of the highest quality is shaped like a stylized squash. Two small square handles project from the neck.

VASE WITH COVER IN SAPPHIRE

Height 9 in. This piece is carved from a single block of pure, translucent sapphire. Peony flowers and phoenixes are carved in high relief on the body, and the handles at the sides of the neck reproduce the "thunder" motif.

92

VASE WITH COVER IN WHITE JADE

Height 7 ½ in. This piece, made in stone of the highest quality, imitates the form of ancient bronze vases. A stylized dragon motif can be recognized in the handles; the decoration of the base is of a floral type.

VASE WITH HIGH-RELIEF CARVINGS IN WHITE JADE

Height 5 ½ in. This piece has a cover and two "S" handles. At the sides of the body, carved in positive with bats and cloud motifs, are high-relief carvings of the figures of two Immortals; one holds a lotus flower, the other a box.

HANDLED VASE WITH COVER IN JADEITE

Opposite below right: *Height 9 in. This piece was made of the highest quality jadeite. The knob of the cover is carved in the form of a hornless dragon, and the two decorated handles have rings. Although the vase has no other decorations, the purity of the material makes it shine with an effect of magnificence.*

93

CUP IN WHITE JADE

Width 5 1/3 in; height 2 1/2 in. The body of this skillfully made piece is hexagonal with extremely thin walls. The cup rests on a small base that is also hexagonal. The volutes around the geometric-motif handles form two stylized hornless dragons.

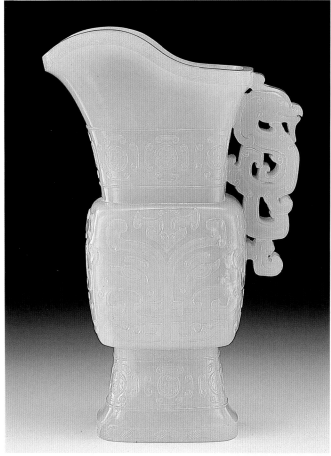

KUNG IN SAPPHIRE

Height 6 1/2 in. This piece is made from sapphire in imitation of ancient bronze containers for rice wine. The handle is in the shape of a dragon; the central part of the kung is decorated with "tao-tie" motifs.

RECTANGULAR VASE IN JADEITE

Height 7 in. The form of this object is very rare. The knob of the cover is in the shape of a incense burner topped by cloud motifs. Phoenixes in low relief stand out from the central part of the body; the neck and two bands at the base are decorated with swastikas (symbol of the sun rolling across the cosmos); the central band of the base bears carved waves.

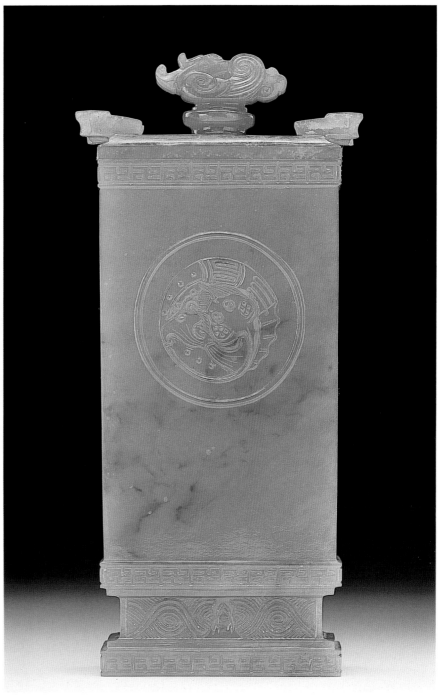

VASE IN JADEITE IN IMITATION OF A KU

Left: Height 4½ in. This magnificent piece is designed on the model of the bronze ku, a container for rice wine. The decorations reproduce banana leaves and motifs similar to those of "tao-tie."

95

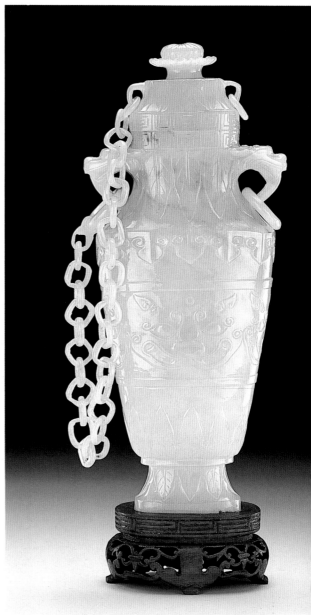

FLOWER VASE WITH SQUASH, LEAVES, AND CRICKET IN JADEITE

Height 8 in. This piece was made during the period that followed the middle period of the Qing dynasty. The cricket, vividly carved on the neck of the vase, is in proportion to the squash and leaves that decorate the body.

VASE WITH COVER IN JADEITE

Height 6½ in. This piece was carved from a single block of stone. A lion holding a branch is carved in full relief on the cover, and the vase's body is decorated with zoomorphic figures and cloud motifs with a pearl from which hangs a cosmic lion with a flaming tail—all symbols of good luck.

VASE WITH CHAIN IN JADEITE

Opposite top right: *Height 7 in. This piece was carved of stone of a clear color in imitation of covered bronze vases. Carved into the body are motifs of clouds, banana leaves, and fanciful and symmetrical lines that recall the idea of the "tao-tie." The two handles that project from the neck and the two that project from the cover are decorated with rings, and the two parts of the vase are joined by a chain that connects the two rings on one side. The knob of the cover is in the form of a chrysanthemum.*

KETTLE IN ROCK CRYSTAL

Height 5 ¾ in. This piece has a square shape. The cover is decorated with floral carvings, the handle is in the shape of the "thunder" motif, and animalistic and cloud motifs decorate the spout. The body carving depicts a pomegranate; the bands at the cover and neck and base are decorated with a geometric design symbolic of infinity.

VASE WITH COVER IN CRYSTAL

Opposite: *Height 18⅓ in. This piece is an imitation of ancient Chinese bronzes. Its form is elegant and richly decorated; among the various fanciful motifs are monster heads with rings on the vase and its cover, palm leaves on the feet of the vase, and the motif of infinity at the mouth and base.*

INCENSE BURNER IN ROCK CRYSTAL

Height 22½ in. This piece was made of a material of great clarity. The various decorated levels are arranged upon one another like towers, and at the top is carved a stylized squash that constitutes the knob of the elegant and thickly worked cover. On the two central bands are carvings of human figures within small frames. A small bell hangs from each of the two circular handles.

INCENSE BURNER WITH TRIPARTITE BASE

Height 8½ in. This piece in rock crystal is a work of remarkable sculptural quality considering the extreme hardness of the mineral from which it was made. It was used for interior decoration. The knob of the cover is rounded. The handles are in the form of monster heads, a ring hanging from each of them, and the body rests on three claw feet.

VASE WITH COVER IN ROCK CRYSTAL

Opposite: *Height 11½ in. This piece is in transparent rock crystal of the highest quality. The two handles on the sides of the neck extend from the gaping jaws of monsters, and each handle encloses a decorated ring. The body is smooth, while the cover has a carved knob.*

INCENSE BURNER WITH LION KNOB IN ROCK CRYSTAL

Height 9⅓ in. This piece is carved in shiny, transparent rock crystal. Rings hang from the handles of the cover and the body, which rests on three feet with an effect of solemnity and stability.

A small, precious world

The figurines carved of jade in human forms during the Qing period, in particular during the reign of Qian Long (1736-96), were the fruit of an ancient tradition, a tradition that adapted itself over time to changing circumstances, to the most various customs, and to the necessities imposed by rites and other demands. The human figures that are present in the Chinese tradition of artistic production often offer us the chance to make accurate reconstructions of how fashions changed over time. They also offer us representations of divinities (most of all Buddha or Bodhisattva) and the clear demonstration of how a religious belief influenced Buddhism, so much so as to change the gender of a divinity, which went from being male to being female, a symbol of motherhood. But we should proceed in an orderly fashion.

From the most remote times, the Chinese believed that another life began after death, a life more or less similar to the life left behind in terms of needs, services, and customs; in this kingdom of the shadows, located near the yellow springs, each person led a life equivalent to that lived on earth. Thus the king would continue to rule, and the slave to serve. In the historical period called by the Chinese the period of slavery, which coincides with the historical period of the Shang dynasty and the early Zhou period, dating to around the 2nd millennium B.C. and the first half of the 1st millennium B.C., a certain number of slaves were buried in the tombs of kings or lords, usually those who had served the dead in life. Traces of this barbarous custom are furnished by the presence of metal rings around the ankles of skeletons. Even after death they had to present themselves to their lord with the marks of captivity, so that there would be no doubts about their condition as slaves.

During the second half of the 1st millennium B.C., a profound process of change within Chinese society led to the abolition of slavery. In tombs, the bodies of slaves along with those persons who in life had served the lords were replaced by life-size terracotta figures, made with great naturalness—artistic representations of the people who in other times had been killed beside the corpse of the lord. Since these terracotta figures did not involve the execution of people it was easy to augment the number of slaves and servants destined to assist the kings and lords in the kingdom of the shadows. Famous

and well-known worldwide are the terracotta statues of soldiers making up the army of the emperor Qinshi Hoangdi, dating to the 3rd century B.C., found in ongoing diggings in the area of Xian, in the province of Shaanxi. The magical symbolism deriving from the use of equivalent figures of terracotta in place of corpses was acceptable since this involved a world of mystery, which is to say the world of shadows. A few decades later, another step in the acceptance of the magical nature of these symbols was taken: symbol by symbol, the figures were made in reduced dimensions instead of being life-size. In tombs from the Han period (202 B.C.-

Su Wu pastoral group in white jade. This piece is noteworthy because of the quality of the material and the skillful execution (length 11½ in; height 5½ in). 103

A.D. 220) and onward the terracotta figures are no longer actual life-size but are far smaller, somewhat like dolls. Terracotta was used to make not only these human figures but also tools, carts, even miniature houses, towers, farmyard animals, and so on: thus nothing would be lacking in the world of the hereafter. During the Tang dynasty (618-907) these tomb figurines, called *ming qi* ("luminous objects"), were not only masterpieces of terracotta but represent proof of the progress achieved by the Chinese in the working of clay, for these figurines were covered with stupendous glazes. In the succeeding Song period (960-1278) the use of tomb furnishings continued, as witnessed by the tombs of the Ming emperors (1368-1644), but there are no longer any traces of the *ming qi*, even though the belief in the continuance of life in the kingdom of the shadows remained intact. (The years 1278 to 1368 are not included in this discussion because they were the period of the Mongolian domination, during which dead emperors, princes, and other high magistrates, all of Mongolian extraction, were brought back to their land of origin for burial.)

The statuettes disappeared from the tombs only to reappear in the studies of the literati, no longer made of terracotta but of porcelain, although the materials most sought for the sculptures of figurines were precious woods and jade. The personages being represented were much different from those once made for tombs. Rather than slaves and trusted servants, these were representations of famous philosophers, from Confucius to Lao-tze, figures from mythology, representations of divinities, or at least those venerated as such, from Buddha to Guan Yin. Guan Yin, the terrestrial projection of Buddha himself, is male. During the Mongolian period (1278-1368), the Nestorian heresy spread across all of continental Asia. This was a cult of the Madonna as the mother of Christ as a man, not a god; thus she was a mother dramatically upset by a tragedy without name and without comfort or divine assistance. Never had a mother been tested as much as the mother of Christ. From this a cult grew around the woman who had suffered all this out of her boundless love for humanity, being consenting and conscious of the tremendous destiny that awaited her. Into this woman was projected motherhood, and she became a symbol of universal love. This cult affected Buddhism. Guan Yin, the male who in his quality of Bodhisattva of

compassion incarnates the image of universal love, underwent a slow process of sweetening of expression in an increasingly marked tendency to resemble a woman. This process of transformation became even more evident during the Ming dynasty, favored in this by a new technique introduced in Chinese vases with the working of porcelain, a technique that permitted— rather, demanded, by its very nature—the creation of more sophisticated clothes, with infinite folds and flourishes, with all the effects suitable for relating the softness of materials. Logically enough, feminine figures were needed to be dressed in such clothes, figures for which there was a market, for which there was a demand: Guan Yin fit this demand. The new technique was called "blanc de Chine." With it were created stupendous female figures of Guan Yin, a symbol ideally suited for these artistic figurations, with mantles of rich flourishes and folds and expressions of particular sweetness on the face of the mother as well as on that of her son, who appeared in her arms.

This was the image that reached jade sculptors during the Qing period. Those artists, as has already been seen, loved to attentively study the products of the past, of which they would make imitations, although they held in their hands a material much different from the ancient bronzes or pieces of porcelain that inspired them. Working in precious and semiprecious stones, from jade to crystal, they reintroduced the fashion that had had a certain success in the Song period, that of sculptures of figurines in jade. The breadth of examples had grown in a notable manner, and there was much food for fancy. The various precious stones used for the carving of the figurines contributed to an increase in their beauty, mystery, and magic, and to that end the creators of these figures used the infinite luminous transparencies, the extemporaneous colors of the minerals, the apparent softness of the waxy surfaces, and naturally, their own great skill as sculptors to create the folds of cloth, the feminine movements (the fashion grew even for the representation of dancers with fluttering veils): they used a thousand artifices to exploit to the highest levels the intrinsic beauty of the minerals. The Qing sculptors, and in particular those of the reign of Qian Long, created what are perhaps the most beautiful jade figurines that have ever been made. That skill, never surpassed, remains as testimony of a golden period in the working of jade.

**STATUE OF THE BODHISATTVA
GUAN YIN IN JADEITE**

*Height 21 ¼ in. The Bodhisattva holds a scepter in his
hand. At his feet is a feminine figure with a fan of palm
leaves. The style was inspired by that of the period of the
Northern Wei (5th-6th centuries).*

STATUE OF BODHISATTVA

Height 7¼ in. This piece is finely carved from white-and-green jadeite. The Bodhisattva is barefoot and holds a pitcher; the draping of his clothing has been rendered vividly. The lion at his side is a symbol of the domination of violence. The Bodhisattva shown here may be Manjusri.

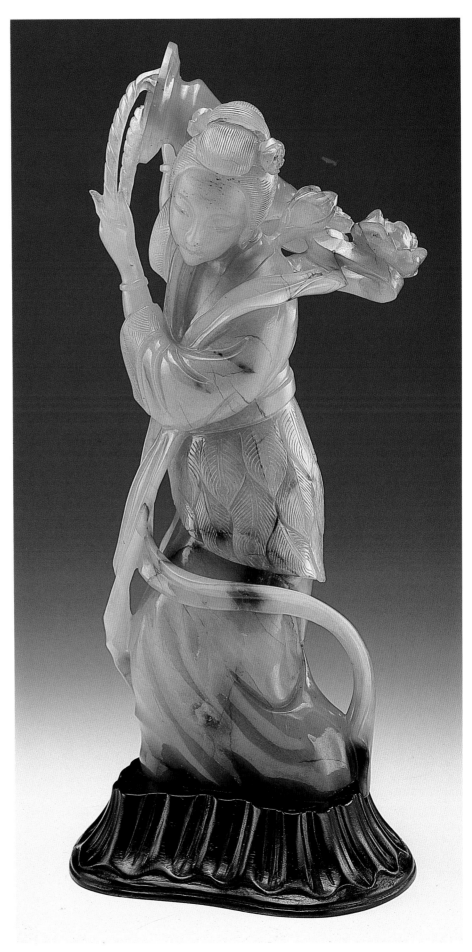

CELESTIAL MAIDEN DISTRIBUTING FLOWERS

Height 9⅓ in. This piece in white-and-green jadeite was worked with notable skill. The celestial maiden, presented with great formal elegance, bears a basket of lotus flowers on her shoulder. The area of her tunic beneath the waist is decorated with a leaf pattern.

STATUETTE OF MU KU

Opposite: *Height 18 in. This piece in gray-green jadeite presents Mu Ku holding a container for rice wine. The bands that extend from the clothing are carved in the form of peach branches. This statuette was used as a decorative object on the occasion of a noblewoman's birthday.*

FIGURE OF BUDDHA IN WHITE JADE

Height 9⅓ in. This statuette is finely carved with great stylistic freedom and perfect balance. The Sakyamuni Buddha is portrayed in meditation, seated in the lotus position: the figure has a sense of absolute serenity.

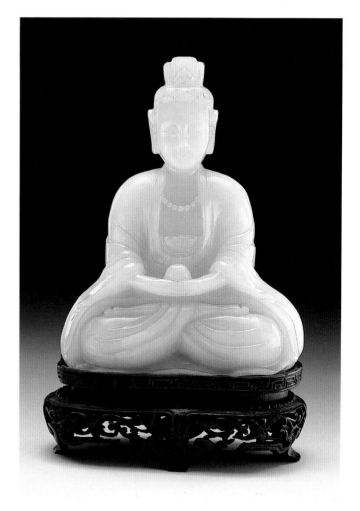

STATUE OF GUAN YIN IN JADEITE

Height 10 in. The feminine Bodhisattva Guan Yin is shown barefoot and holding a scepter (ruyi). Her face expresses great sweetness. The figures of two praying children are carved at her sides.

STATUE OF THE BODHISATTVA GUAN YIN IN JADEITE

Opposite: Height 15¾ in. This representation of the Bodhisattva Guan Yin follows the common sculptural model for female figures of the middle period of the Qing dynasty. The styles of the hair and clothing are similar to those of the common people.

FEMALE FIGURE IN WHITE JADE

Height 6 in. This sculpture is carved of the finest quality material. The noblewoman bears a chest on her arm and holds a lotus flower in her hand. Her bearing is tranquil and serene. The execution of the draping of her clothing is of particular skill.

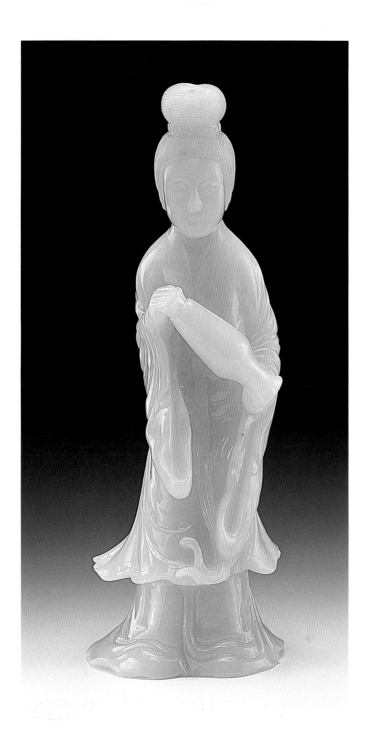

STATUE OF NOBLEWOMAN IN WHITE JADE

Height 8¾ in. The softness and smoothness of the white jade of which this female figure is carved are in perfect harmony with the serenity of her appearance. The woman holds a vase. The execution of the folds of the clothing is admirable.

110

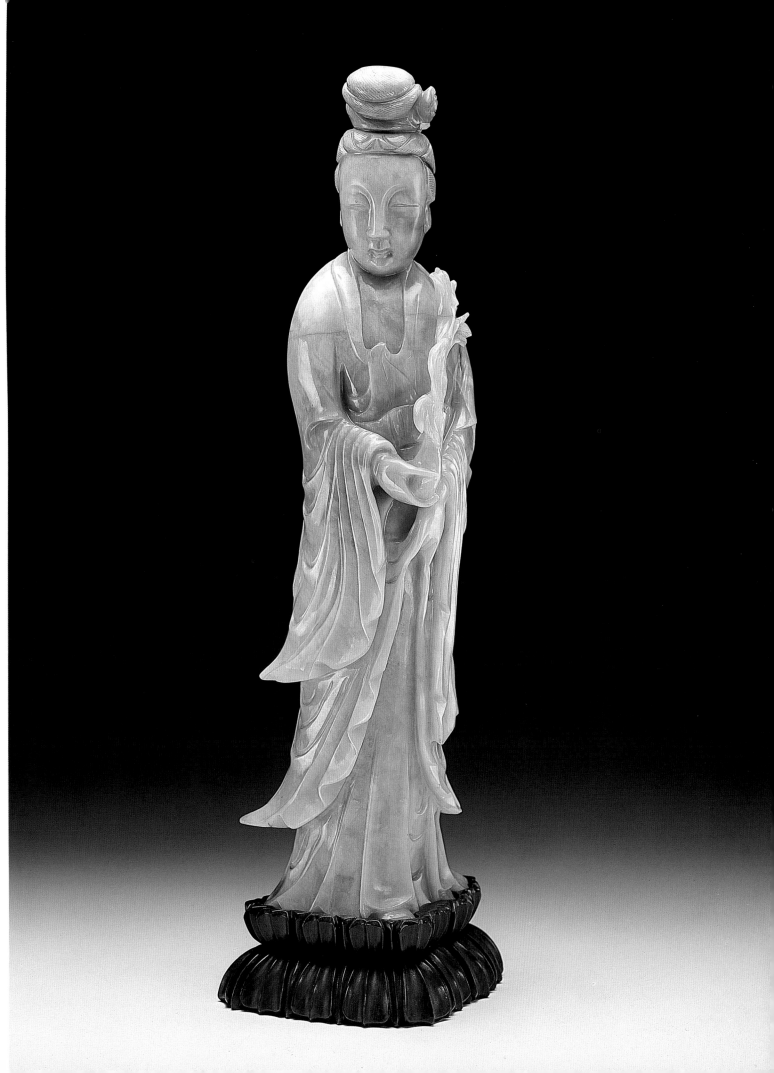

FIGURES OF MASCULINE AND FEMININE DIVINITIES

Height 9 in. This piece is finely carved in white jadeite. The two figures, inspired by Taoism, are shown on the foam of sea waves.

FIGURE OF YOUNG GIRL IN JADEITE

Height 8½ in. The flowering, leafy branches in the hands of the young girl indicate she is a symbolic harbinger of spring.

STATUE OF GUAN YIN IN JADEITE

Height 15¾ in. The Bodhisattva holds a small vase with a branch in his right hand; with his left he makes a gesture symbolic of averting evil.

FIGURE OF IMMORTAL GIRL IN JADEITE

Height 9⅓ in. The unusual position of movement, emphasized by the fluttering of the clothing, is achieved with notable mastery.

113

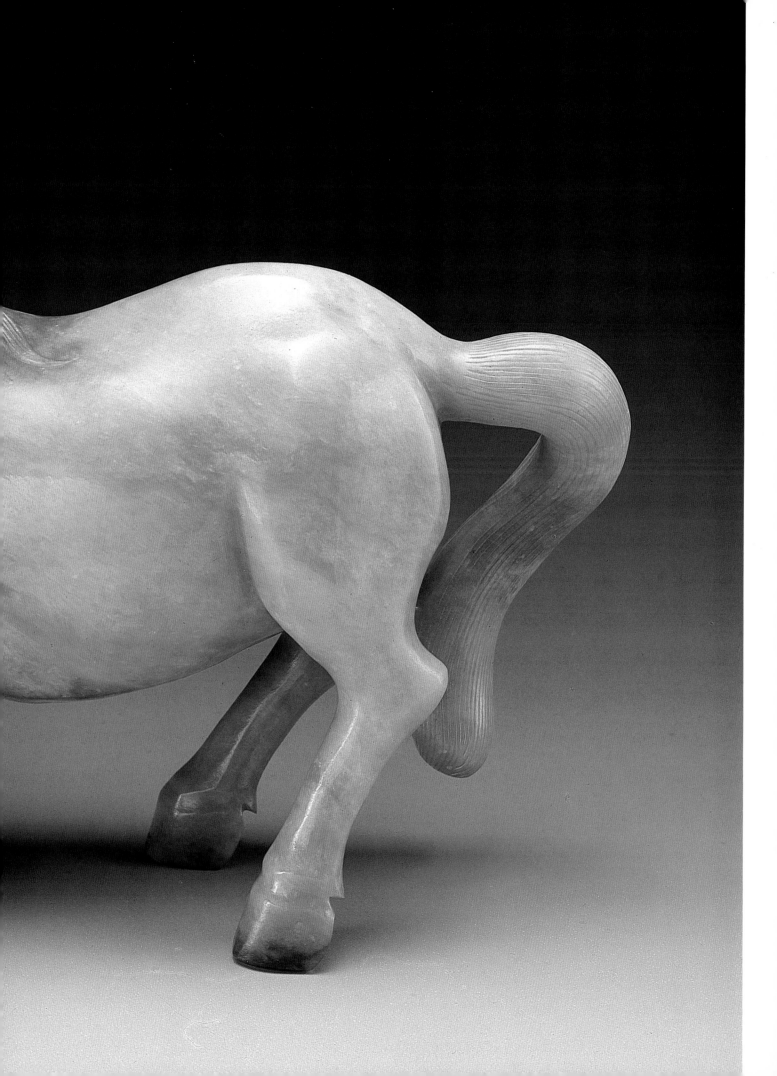

BOY PULLING A HORSE

Preceding pages (114-15): *Width 8⅓ in; height 4½ in. This piece was made from a single block of green jadeite. The boy has grasped the reins of the spirited horse and is trying to pull it.*

STATUETTE OF GUAN GUN IN JADEITE

Opposite: *Height 5¼ in. This piece in soft green jadeite shows Guan Gun seated and dressed in military clothing. He holds a book entitled Jun Qiù in his left hand and caresses his beard with his right. The expression on his face is one of satisfaction.*

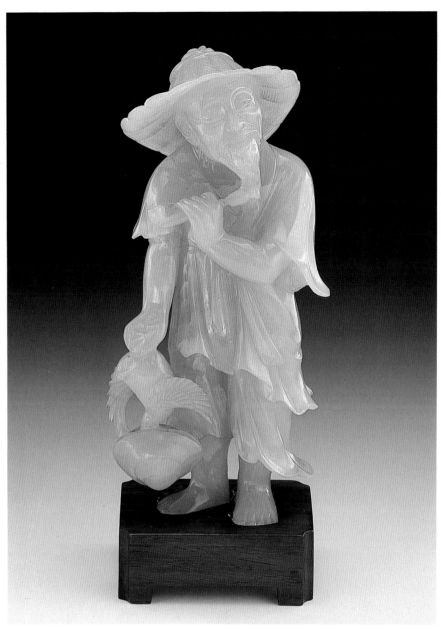

MALE FIGURE IN SAPPHIRE

Height 4½ in. This piece, carved of stone of the best quality, represents a man in humble clothing wearing a bamboo hat. In his left hand he holds a pipe, and in his right a bird, the head of which is closed in a seashell, perhaps a symbol of abundance.

STATUE OF JI GUN IN WHITE JADE

Left: *Height 9⅓ in. This piece represents Ji Gun, an extraordinary monk of the Song period. He holds a container of rice wine in one hand and a palm-leaf fan in the other.*

STATUE OF THE BODHISATTVA GUAN YIN

Opposite: Height 12½ in. This piece is carved of white-and-green jadeite. The folds of the clothing and the wide sleeves are vividly carved. The Bodhisattva Guan Yin smiles. At the top of her head she wears a jeweled ornament and around her neck a necklace of precious stones. She holds a bowl in her left hand, and her right is raised in front of her chest in a gesture of benediction.

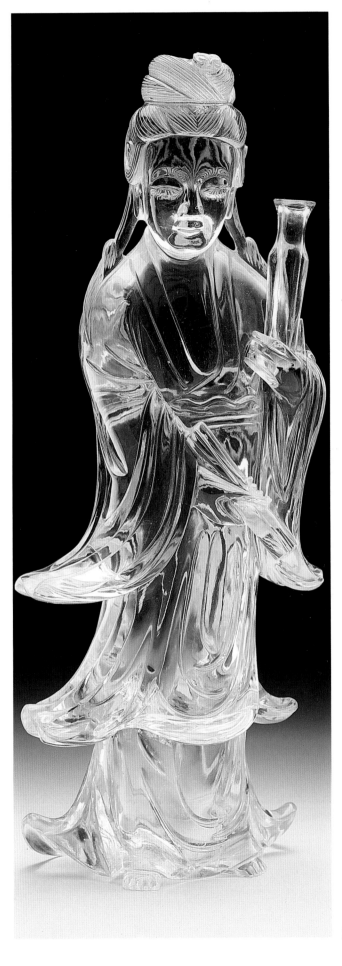

FEMININE FIGURE IN ROCK CRYSTAL

Height 11 in. This piece is carved in extremely fine rock crystal. The overlapping folds of the clothing and the wide sleeves seem to move in the air and give an impression of movement. The woman's hair is gathered atop her head in the form of a high chignon; she holds a vase in her left hand.

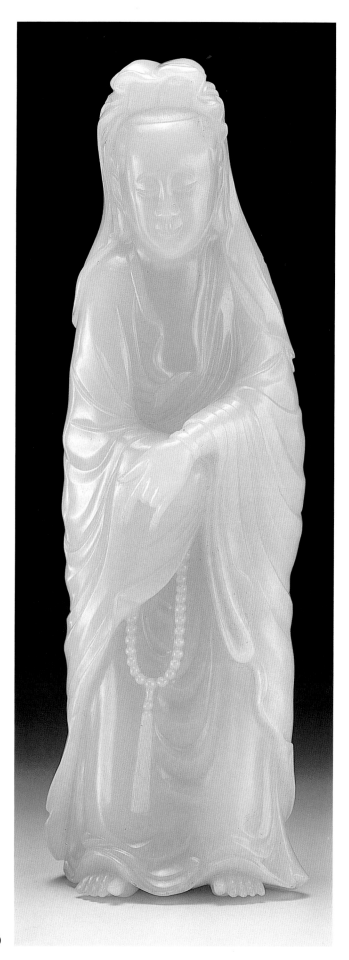

STATUETTE OF THE BODHISATTVA GUAN YIN IN WHITE JADE

Height 9 in. This piece was made with great skill during the last period of the Qing dynasty: Guan Yin stands barefoot and holds a rosary. The figure of the Bodhisattva emanates gentility and dignity.

STATUETTE OF GUAN YIN IN JADEITE

Height 8 in. This piece is carved in white-and-pink jadeite. The large Victoria leaves and lotus bud attest to purity. The overall harmony of the piece is superb.

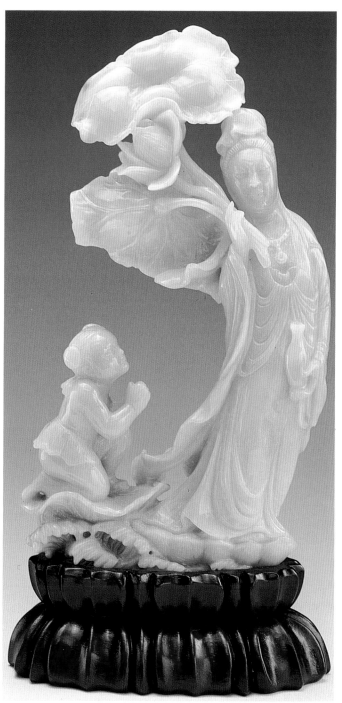

FIGURE OF GUAN YIN IN JADEITE

Height 8⅓ in. This piece is made from white-and-green jadeite. The Bodhisattva is shown in a somewhat unusual position that emphasizes the "realism" sought by the artist; as is traditional, she holds a small bottle in her left hand.

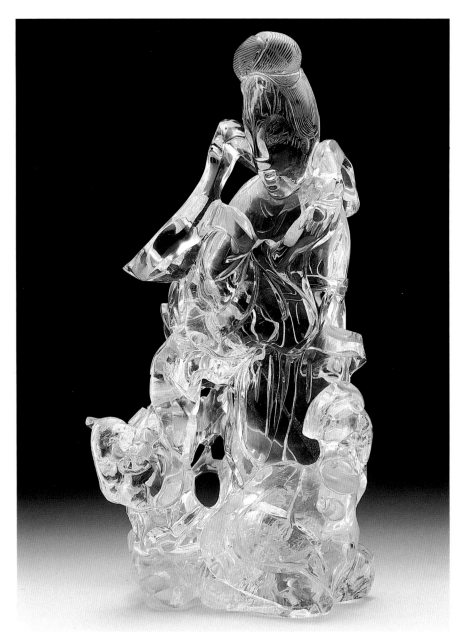

STATUE OF BODHISATTVA IN CRYSTAL

Height 10 ½ in. This piece is a work of great sculptural value. The Bodhisattva has a whip on his shoulders. The lion crouching in front of him indicates that this figure represents Manjusri: to subdue a lion means to overcome violence.

STATUE OF THE BODHISATTVA GUAN YIN

Height 13 ½ in. This piece was made of rock crystal by a capable artist. The Bodhisattva bears a rosary and appears serene and full of dignity.

FIGURE OF AN OLD MAN IN TURQUOISE

Height 5 in. This piece was made from a single block of turquoise. The smiling old man gathers flowers while sitting on a stone chair with his legs crossed. Behind him is a pine, and beneath the stone chair are flowering chrysanthemums.

RECLINING ARHAT TAMING A LION

Height 7 in. This piece made in steatite is excellent both because of its overall effect and the skill of its execution. It shows a half-reclining emaciated arhat (Buddhist "saint"), who emanates serenity and beatitude. In one hand he holds a rosary. Beside him is a small lion that looks up at him.

STATUETTE OF SEATED MAITREYA BUDDHA

Height 4 in. This piece is of very hard rock crystal of great purity. The bare-chested Maitreya Buddha is seated next to an incense burner set on a stone shelf. The smoke of the incense rises in the air to form a cloud.

124

EAGLES IN JADEITE

Height 5¼ in. Two eagles, one large and one small, are perched on branches and facing each other. The capable execution presents a realistic situation.

PAIR OF PHOENIXES IN JADEITE

Height 7¼ in; width 5¼ in. Each phoenix is carved from a block of jadeite. The two birds are carved with a capable and elaborate technique. They hold peony branches in their beaks and are symbols of good fortune.

PAIR OF PARROTS

Height 7½ in. This piece, skillfully carved in green jadeite, shows a mother parrot with her offspring resting against her chest. The mother holds a peach branch in her beak. The group is a symbol of good fortune and motherly love.

PARROT IN JADEITE

Below: Height 3¼ in. This piece shows a parrot perched on branches; it is carved in green jadeite with brown streaks, and the artist capably exploited the variations in the colors of the stone to realistically render the subject. Slight linear carving adds further naturalness to the work.

PAIR OF CRANES IN JADEITE

Height 6¼ in; width 5½ in. The two cranes (divine birds), slender and pretty, stand with their heads and necks turned backward; each holds a fern in its beak, symbol of good luck.

126

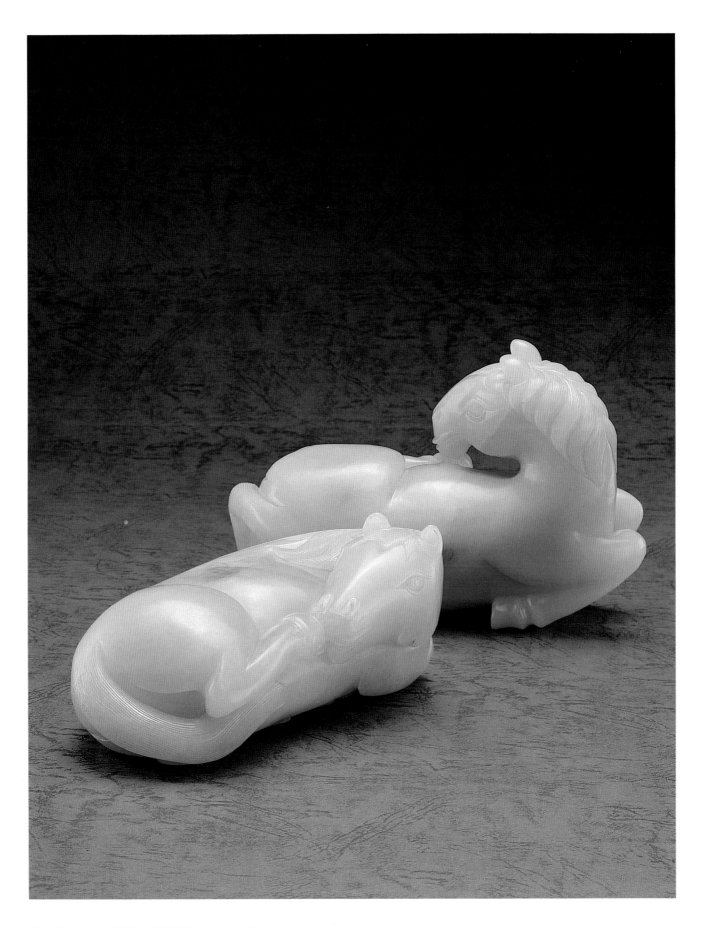

PAIR OF HORSES IN WHITE JADE

Length 7 in. Following a widespread model, these two horses are posed as though in the wild.

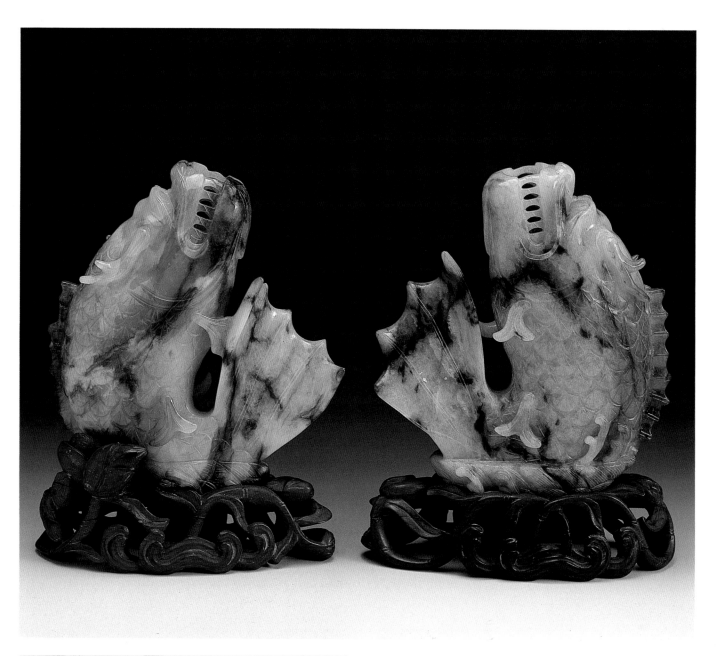

PAIR OF FISH-SHAPE FLOWER VASES

Height 6 in. These two pieces, carved in gray-green jade, are similar to carp. Flowers could be inserted in the openings of their toothed mouths; their tails are spread like fans. The color of the stone reproduces very well the colors and natural reflections of carp.

ZOOMORPHIC FIGURE IN WHITE JADE

Length 5⅓ in; height 4½ in. The white jade of this piece is splendid because of its quality and shine. The shape of the animal indicates that it was made in a period later than the Qing and Ming dynasties. The animal holds a peony flower in its jaws.

GROUP OF GOATS IN JADEITE

Length 4-5 in. The two larger pieces with horns curved like rams are carved of black stone; the pair of smaller figures, with straight horns, are carved from white jadeite.

FISH-SHAPED BOX IN SAPPHIRE

Length 6 in. The fish resembles a carp; the motif of the little waves that surround the fish at the base and the lotus flowers carved at its sides suggest the idea of a fish swimming in a pond. This object served as a jewelry box.

DUCK IN ROCK CRYSTAL

Length 6 in. This piece presents a bird that has caught a fish and holds it in its beak. The animal rests on a base carved to represent water. The object is a table ornament.

LION IN ROCK CRYSTAL

Length 5 ¼ in. This piece is carved from a piece of clear, transparent rock crystal. The lion is resting with an air of peaceful satisfaction. The object served as a decorative element in the study of a man of letters.

DEER IN CITRINE

Length 5 ½ in. This piece has elegant lines and form, and the figure is rendered in a lively manner. The body is yellow, and the tail has reddish reflections, perhaps to indicate that the animal is wounded.

130

DRAGON IN ROCK CRYSTAL

Height 9 in. This piece is finely carved of brown rock crystal with yellow shadings and great clarity. The dragon is perched on a sphere and has its jaws open. The base is in the form of a turbulent wave.

FIGURES OF GOATS

Length 7½ in. This piece of great artistic value is carved in white-and-pink jadeite. One
of the goats is drinking water that, following a twisting route, comes from distant clouds.

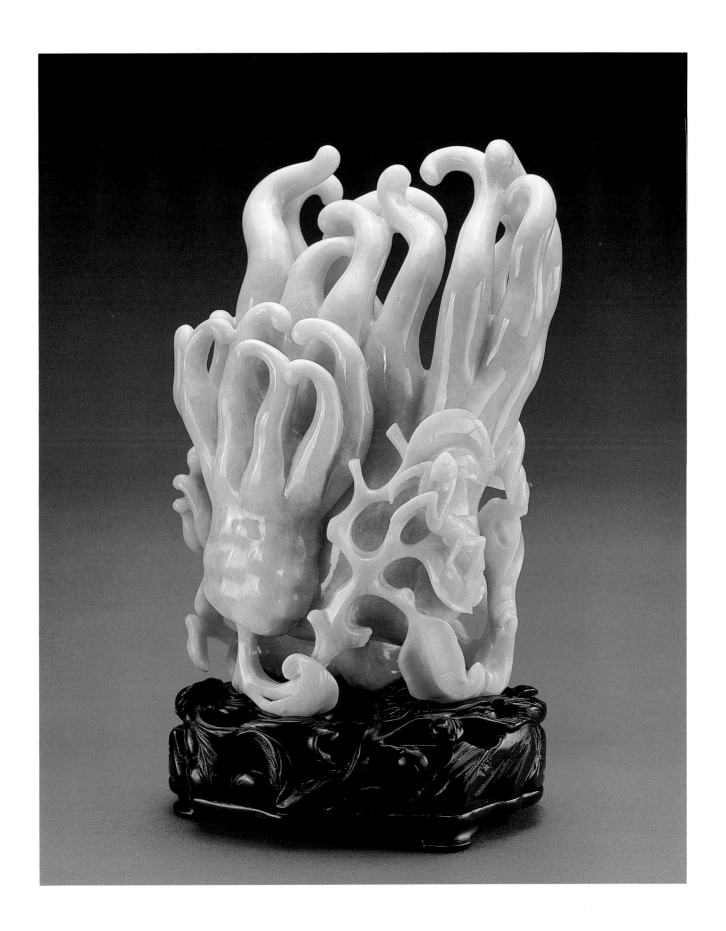

HAND OF BUDDHA IN JADEITE

Height 8 in. This piece of great formal originality is made from jadeite of various colors, including white, pink, and green.

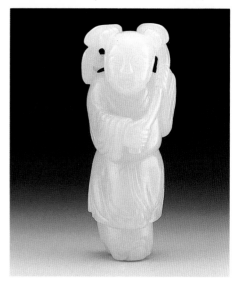

FIGURINES IN JADE

Height 1 1/2-3 in. Although of minuscule size, these decorative objects display excellent workmanship. The lines of the small human figures made of white jade and green jade are sculpted and carved with skill.

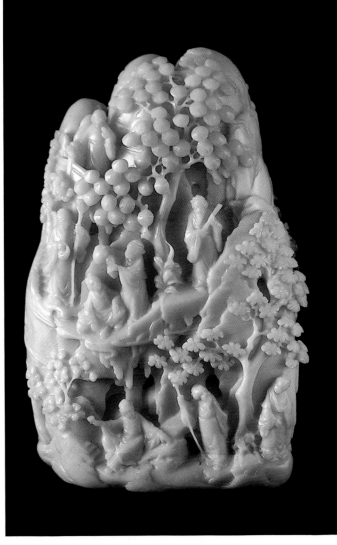

MOUNTAIN LANDSCAPE WITH GROUP OF SCHOLARS

Height 8 in. This piece in white-and-pink jadeite presents a group of scholars immersed in nature. Their figures stand out amid elegant conifers that rise on various levels of the mountain.

The scepter, symbol of power

If there is an object that seems destined to be carved of jade, it is the scepter, which the Chinese call *ruyi*. And yet, if there is an object that has been worked in all the possible materials, this too is the scepter. Scepters can be found made of molded or carved gold, silver, wood, bamboo, horn, ivory, jade, stone, ceramics, and porcelain. It is difficult to find an object that had a greater fortune than the *ruyi* in the artistic and symbolic Chinese tradition. In fact, because of this object's strong symbolic force and its basic form it has always been well suited to the highest creativity and the greatest whims of artists. The term *ruyi*, does not mean "scepter," but means instead "as you wish," since *ru* means "as," "in the same manner in which," and *yi* means "desire." Naturally, the desire to be fulfilled belongs to the person to whom the *ruyi* is given as a gift. Because of this sense of being a symbol of good luck for the receiver, the *ruyi* is a typical gift item. To acquire one for oneself would make no sense. The meaning comes into being only when it is something given as a gift. It is a gift made to be given to all people, from friends and relatives all the way up the social scale to the emperor. In point of fact, the *ruyi* is the gift high dignitaries at court offered the emperor after the prescribed number of *go dou* bows; to the emperor one might offer a *ruyi* of refined handiwork, carved in the purest jade. In such cases, aside from the meaning just described, which is to say the hope that everything goes just as the emperor wishes, there is also the intrinsic value of the jade, the preciousness of which becomes a symbol of purity both on the part of the giver and on that of the recipient.

The origin of the *ruyi* as a scepter to be given as a gift has been lost in time. Its form appears in the period known as the Six Dynasties (318-581), but in the beginning it was only a decorative element, carved at the base of stone monuments. It appears immediately later as a decorative element in paintings as well; the shape of the *ruyi* taken altogether is pretty much uniform, even if it has been the subject of variations of notable importance. What always varies, from one scepter to another, is the decoration. The *ruyi* is composed of two parts: a head and a handle, as necessary for a scepter. Taken altogether, its form is that of a hooked baton, in which the hook is what makes up the head of the scepter. The head is circular or lobate, slightly larger than the handle, which is always flat and rarely round, but always characterized by a slight arched curvature in the middle. During the Qing period, because of the great burst of jade sculpture and the fashionable reappearance of certain symbols, *ruyi* experienced a new popularity, and the variety that the artists gave the form was so great that in some cases it is difficult to recognize its origins: the changes done to the original model are so great that the scepter nearly disappears. As an example, the head is sometimes multiplied. We have *ruyi* with two, three, and even five heads. Carved in jade, with inlays of other precious stones, the *ruyi* ended up becoming objects of display, very different from their origins, and eventually they lost their symbolic value to those venal, represented by the richness of the work and the preciousness of the objects from which they were derived. The decoration of the *ruyi* is of an incredible variety, and naturally it too contributes to the enrichment of the object and its symbolic meaning. The most common decoration carved for the head consists of broken-up volutes that recall the wrapping of vines; of clouds; or waves of the sea. The handle, well-suited to decoration because it is long and flat, can be the scene of carvings of plum branches, with flowers and leaves wrapping around the handle and ending in a twisted mass of roots at the bottom, conferring fineness and elegance to an image of decorum and adding the value of further good wishes (the plum is a symbol of youth). The decorative variants are infinite, and each scepter must be examined and analyzed in its values and its symbols, case by case. Very widespread were the scepters made of precious wood, usually black, finely carved and pierced like a work of needlepoint, into which were set small, thin blocks of jade, also carved with extreme fineness and beauty. The head is rounded or lobate, while the jade blocks applied to the handle, carved rectangles, are in the form of small human sculptures, showing historical characters of great importance, such as ancient philosophers or figures drawn from myth. The handle is slightly curved toward the center so as to take on a trace of movement that is then created in the shape of the head. The length of the *ruyi* is more or less that of a forearm, because in the moment of being offered it was held leaning against the left forearm. The *ruyi* is too special and too interesting, not to mention too precious, to have escaped the attention of European collectors. In this sense there are many important private collections, although it is not easy to find important holdings in European state museums.

SCEPTER (RUYI) IN JASPER

Length 17½ in. This piece, made in green jasper, is rather long and has a handle decorated with floral and leaf motifs. The head bears a carving of clouds.

139

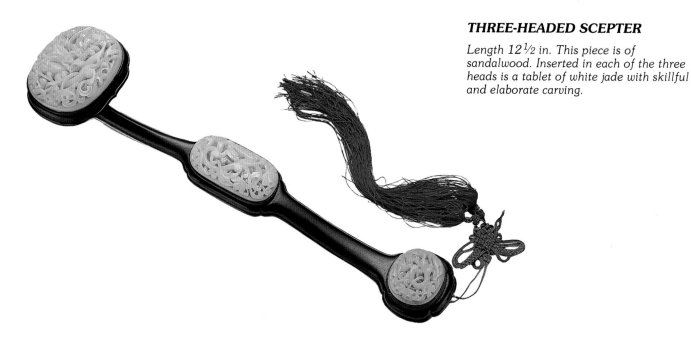

THREE-HEADED SCEPTER

*Length 12½ in. This piece is of
sandalwood. Inserted in each of the three
heads is a tablet of white jade with skillful
and elaborate carving.*

SCEPTER IN SANDALWOOD WITH
INLAID WHITE JADE

*Length 19 in. Inserted in the almost
circular head of this scepter is a very
elegant tablet in white jade carved with a
Zhou character and with the images of
some of the "eight jewels." The tip of the
handle is inlaid with a carving of clouds and
bats, symbols of good luck.*

SCEPTER IN WHITE-GREEN JADEITE

Length 16 in; width 5 in. The head and handle of this piece are finely carved in relief with motifs of peach branches.

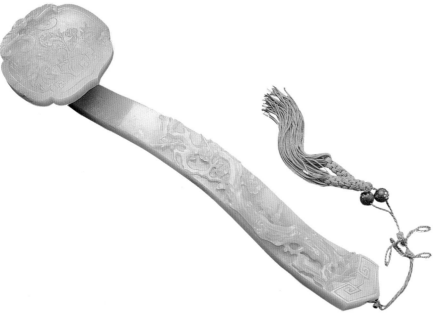

SCEPTER IN WHITE JADE

Length 17 in. The handle of this object has decoration in relief showing a plum tree. Carved in the head are motifs of bats and flowering plants, symbols of wealth and good luck.

SCEPTER IN STEATITE

Length 13½ in. This piece was carved from a single block of steatite following a procedure similar to that used for wood. It is completely covered with decorations of plum flowers and intertwining roots.

SCEPTER IN SAPPHIRE

Length 15½ in. The head of this piece bears carvings showing rocks and pine trees. The elegant decoration with the motif of pines is repeated on the handle. This object was made to be given as a gift.

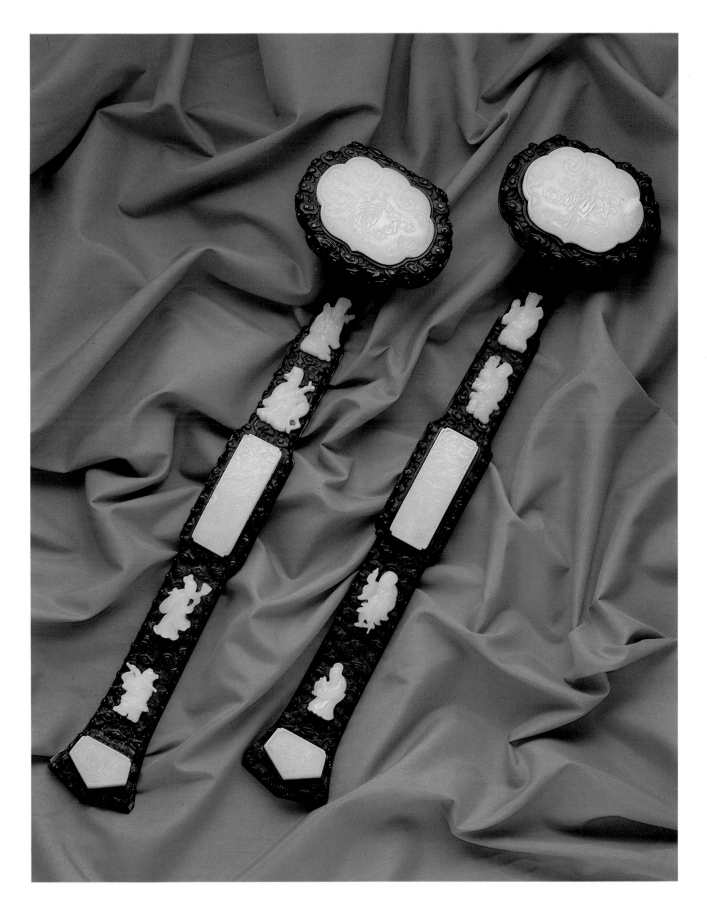

SCEPTERS IN SANDALWOOD WITH INLAID WHITE JADE

Length 17 in. These two pieces are inlaid with pieces of jade finely carved with motifs of clouds and men.
The figurines that stand out on the shafts of the two ruyi, four each, represent the Eight Immortals of Taoism.

御製千尺雪詩

層巖門延出雲嶄

小閣三間迤采几

便與佳名顏聽雪

何當坐此讀華嚴

臣劉大海敬書

On the tables of the literati

The Song period (960-1278) has been defined as the period of the literati, meaning by that term not only those who wrote but also those who painted. Both groups used the brush and ink, and in most cases both activities ended up being performed by the same person. This is why the term *literati* is taken to include both expressions of cultural activity, which are performed with the same instruments: the pen and ink. In earlier times, the term *literati* was used for the political and moral authority sanctioned by official doctrine, meaning Confucianism. The decline of Confucianism, caused by historical forces, was followed by the rise of new doctrines, Taoism and Buddhism, which became widespread and even moved into positions of power, most of all during the 10th century. These doctrines took over an area in Chinese culture. The rise of those doctrines was entwined in the contemporary weakening of Confucianism and the state itself, which had founded its laws on the principles of Confucianism and its management on the bureaucracy of Confucianism. With the Song dynasty began a profound process of revision, of reworking and developing philosophical thinking; this led to the affirmation of a new doctrine, richer than Confucianism and more complex than the individualist doctrines of Taoism and Buddhism. This new doctrine was called neoconfucianism. With the triumph of neoconfucianism rose also the authority of the preeminent position of "literati." As a consequence these literati found themselves with the obligations of a higher style of life. In another chapter, we have seen the birth of the luxury screen made of jade and precious woods artistically carved. The introduction of the screen, so complex and of such costly manufacture, can be considered the consecration of the existence within the home of a study. This led to the necessity of furnishing the study at the height of refined and lordly taste demanded by the screen. Thus we see in the Song period the birth of furnishings that we could call today chancellery or study furnishings.

The materials used by the literati in the performance of their activities had to bear witness to their wealth, power, and refined taste, and for this reason a large portion of the objects made for use in the study were made of jade, to a Confucian, a symbol of virtue.

Following the order of priority, the first indispensable work tool of the literati was, of course, the brush, the holder of which was usually made of wood or cane but could also be made of jade. The literati made use of a large variety of brushes, since it was necessary to create every possible variation of density of line, aside from handling the varying densities of the inks. The various brushes were held together in containers, in cylindrical or prismatic forms, made of wood, bamboo, ivory—and also of jade. Also made of jade were the small brush rests on which the brushes could be laid in turn as they were used and alternated according to the needs of writing or painting. Another essential element were blocks of ink, and the box in which these were held could be made of wood or jade. As for the pages of paper used both for writing and painting, these were held in groups by a paperweight of jade, just as heavier paperweights were used for books; also made of jade were the papercutters. On the table in discussion, together with the blocks of ink there was, naturally, an inkpot, which held water in which to rub the blocks of ink to obtain ink of the desired density: these inkpots were made of hardwood, stone, or jade. There were also on the table sticks of incense in a jade box, and an incense burner to burn them, also of jade. To have near at hand a reserve of water to pour into the inkpot it was necessary to have a container flared for pouring, and this could be made of jade. On one side of the table was the seal of the literatus, with its jade handle, and the ink pad used to impregnate the seal with ink. These instruments made up the necessary basic equipment of a Chinese literatus of the 13th century. There would also be other objects in the interior of the area destined for use as a study by a literatus, those used to embellish the area, such as vases of various size (of porcelain), statuettes of human figures, arm rests, scepters (*ruyi*) received as gifts, symbolic signs of good luck. This study equipment, which is known to have been in use by the literati of the 13th century, continued to be adopted with greater or lesser fortune even during later epochs. But it was during the Qing dynasty, because of all the political situations of the period and the importance of the literati in a phase of resurgent Confucian traditions, and because of the need to make the state strong and well organized, that the old customs of the literati of ancient times were taken up again along with the old pleasures in wealth and the sensibility for what is beautiful, which returned intact to take on new value: the equipment for a study became an integral part of Song furnishings. Obviously, made of jade.

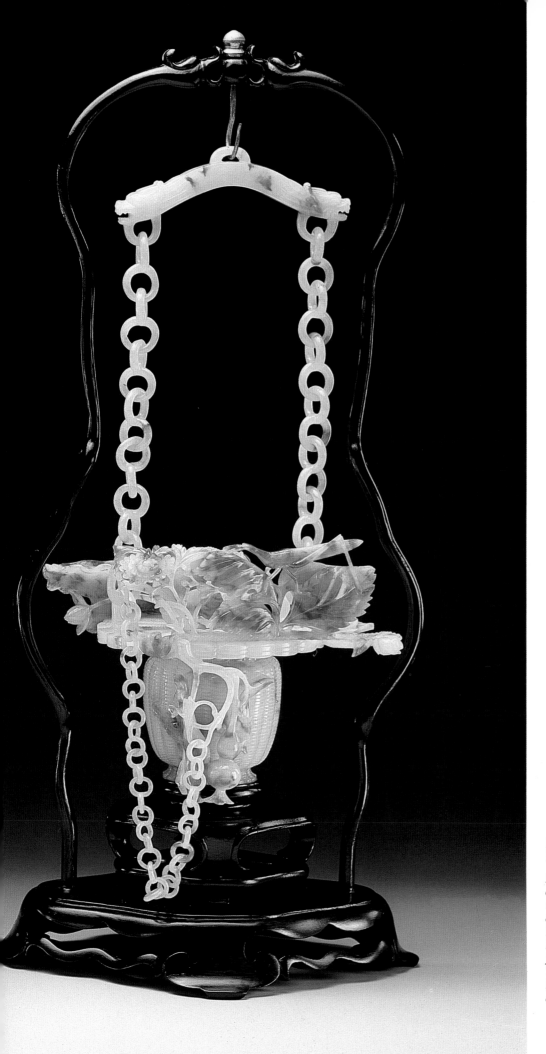

FLOWER BASKETS
IN JADEITE

Height 11½ in. The white-
and-green stone from which
these pieces were carved is
of great quality. The baskets
have ornamental chains and
bear wonderfully carved
flowers, leaves, and crickets.
These are among the most
beautiful jades of the Qing
dynasty.

147

FLOWER VASE IN THE SHAPE OF A CABBAGE

Opposite: *Height 5¼ in. This piece is in white jadeite with green streaks. Two crickets are carved at the top of the leaves of the plant; a radish projects from the base.*

INKSTAND IN THE FORM OF A LOTUS LEAF

Length 5 in. This piece was made from green jadeite during the late period of the Qing dynasty. The exterior part is decorated with elegant lotus-flower motifs, reeds, and birds.

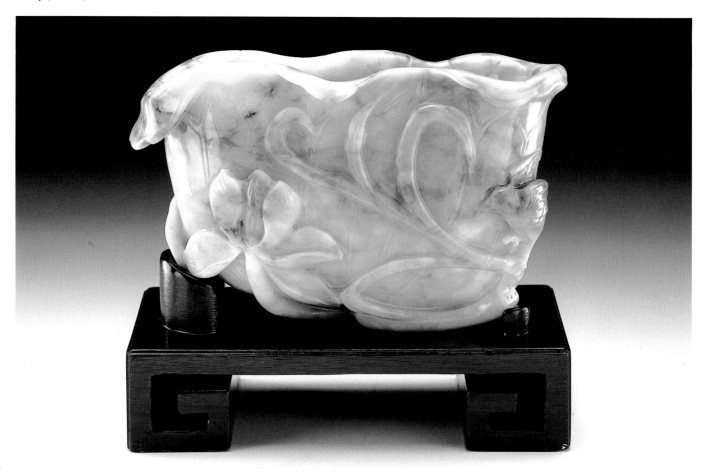

149

DOUBLE-HORN-SHAPED CUP

Width 4 in; height 3 in. This piece, made in white jade, has a tapering base, and the body is decorated with mushrooms of eternity, which also function as support.

FLOWER VASE IN YELLOW JADE

Opposite: Height 5 in. This piece is in the shape of an irregular cylinder: from the wide mouth it narrows toward the base. The body is decorated with vigorous lines that represent both large and small mushrooms of eternity.

DOUBLE FLOWER VASE IN JADEITE

Height 5½ in. The jadeite from which this piece was carved is white with two tones of green streaks. The body is in the shape of bamboo canes and is capably carved in relief with leaves of that plant. The effect is of great elegance.

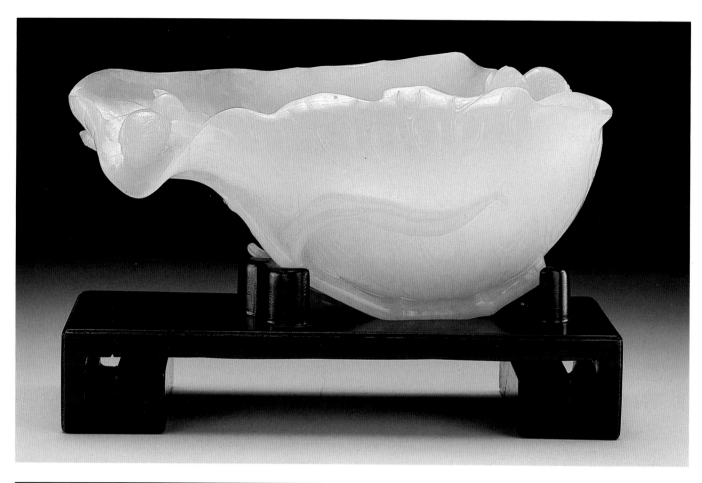

INKSTAND IN WHITE JADE

Left: Length 7 in. This piece was carved from stone of the best quality. It is in the shape of a partly closed lotus leaf supported, at the base, by branches and steles. Two Mandarin ducks are carved at the edge, and the veins of the lotus leaf are carved into the surface.

INKSTAND IN THE FORM OF A LEAF

Length 9 in. This piece was made in gray jade in the shape of a flat leaf. Wave motifs are carved in the inner surface. The edge is decorated with the figure of a hornless dragon.

INKSTAND IN WHITE JADE

Opposite: *Length 6⅓ in. This piece was carved from very fine stone. The artist gave it the shape of a partly open lotus leaf. The body is decorated with the veins of the leaf, and a small bird rests on the edge, where the leaf is slightly bent down.*

INKSTAND IN THE FORM OF A LOTUS

Length 7½ in. This piece (shown below and upside down to the right) was carved from white jade. The lotus leaf seems to be turning in on itself. The decoration is constituted by a frog carved on the inner surface and by motifs of leaves, steles, flowers, and roots of lotus carved on the external surface.

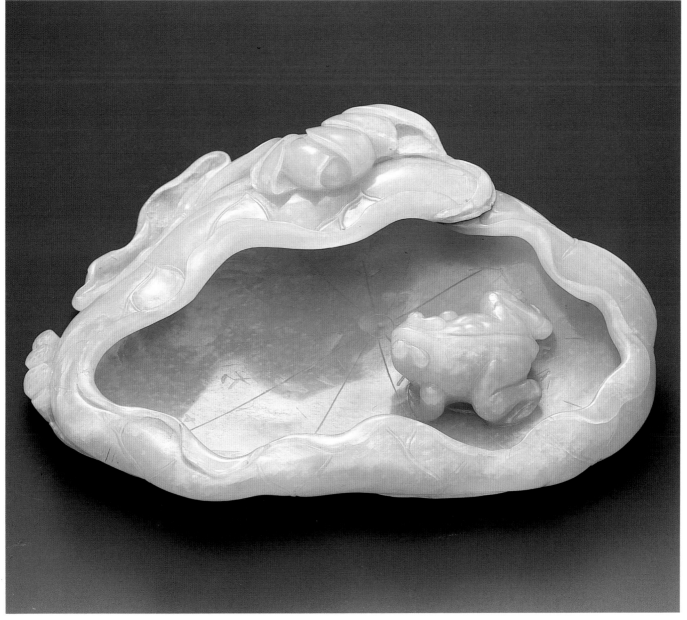

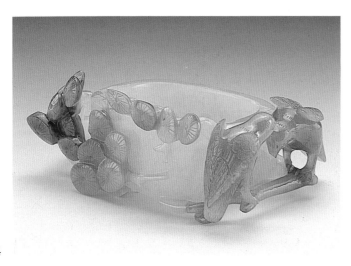

INKSTAND IN JADEITE

Length 7¼ in. This piece, carved from a single block of white-and-green jadeite, represents a lotus leaf decorated with steles and small leaves and seems to be closing slightly.

PINE-TRUNK INKSTAND

Length 3½ in. This piece is finely carved in white-and-green jadeite. The form of the trunk, the two eagles on a branch, one in front of the other, and the many small mushrooms of eternity are created with great artistic skill.

INKSTAND IN JADEITE

Width 5½ in. This piece is fancifully carved: the images of plum branches and magpies are symbols of good luck. The execution of the ornamental motifs is exceptional. The points on the base where the piece rests are decorated with cloud motifs (right).

DOUBLE INKSTAND IN WHITE JADE

Width 8 in; height 3⅓ in. This piece, worked in an uncommon manner, is in the shape of two peaches, one larger than the other, and around the two pieces of fruit are carved mushrooms of eternity.

DOUBLE INKSTAND AND ZOOMORPHIC FIGURE

Length of inkstand 7 in; width of figure 2½ in. The inkstand, shaped like two pieces of fruit with steles and leaves, is made of pink jadeite; the zoomorphic sculpture is in white jade.   157

BRUSH HOLDER IN WHITE JADE

Height 5 3/4 in; diameter 5 1/2 in. The images carved into this piece present literati meeting and walking together through nature. In the foreground shown here can be seen two crossing a bridge over a water course.

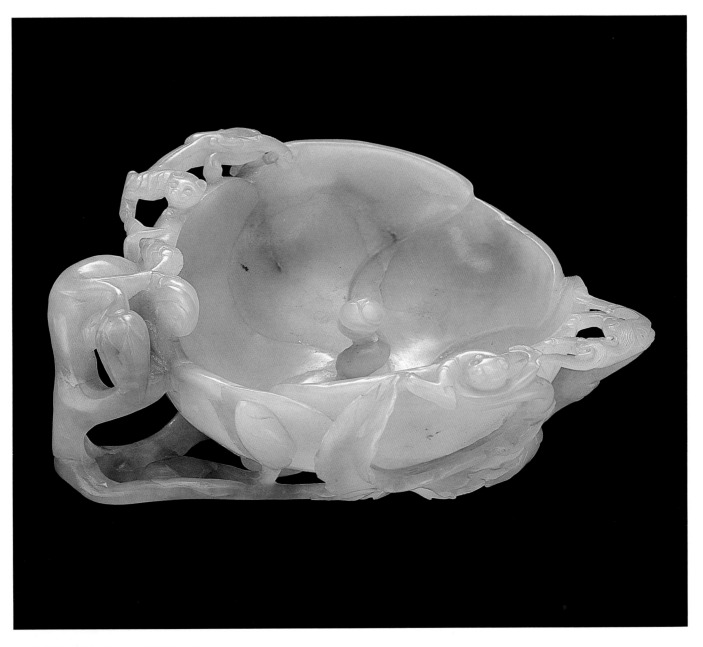

LOTUS-FLOWER INKSTAND

Width 6 in. This piece, shown upside down at right, is made from white jade. Carved into it are two hornless dragons, symbols of good luck. Inkstands were indispensable objects for literati. Some were given as gifts by close friends.

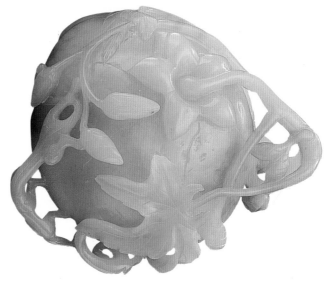

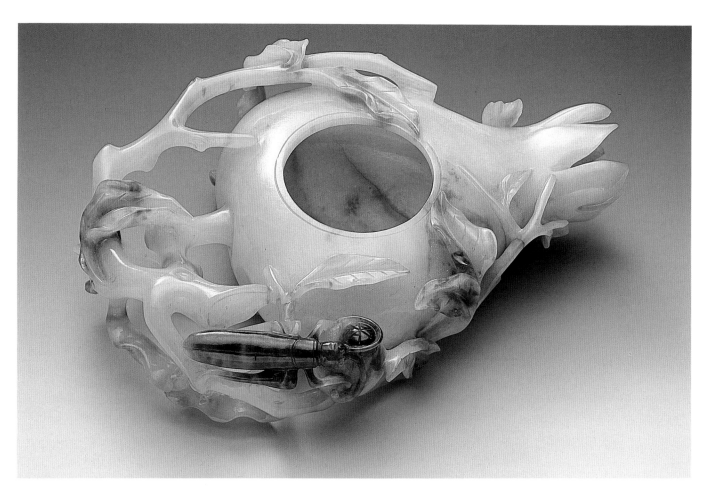

INKSTAND IN THE SHAPE OF A POMEGRANATE

Length 7 in. This piece in white-and-green jadeite is in the shape of a pomegranate and has a circular opening in the center. Carved around the piece of fruit are steles and leaves and among them a cricket.

INKSTAND IN THE SHAPE OF A PEACH

Length 12 in. This piece in white jade is in a shape similar to that of a peach. It has a central round opening, and carved around its body are branches and small peaches. The peach is a symbol of longevity.

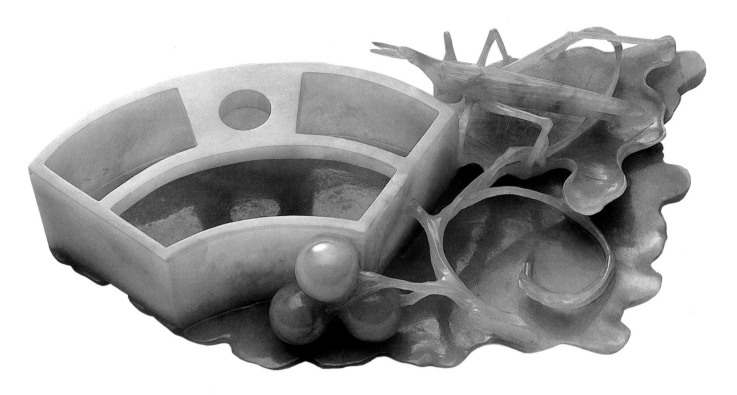

INKSTAND WITH GRAPES AND CRICKET

Length 7⅓ in. This piece is in white-and-green jadeite. On one side is a small fan-shaped reservoir, and on the other are grapes and a cricket on a vine leaf.

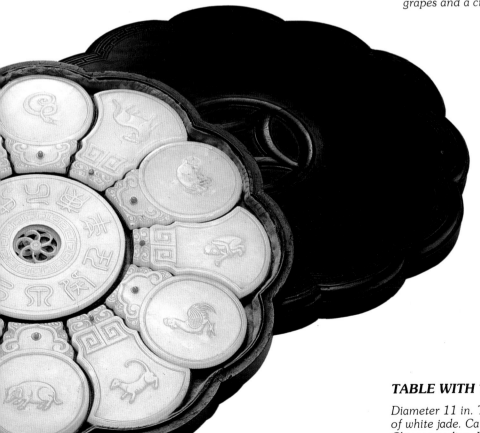

TABLE WITH THE ANIMALS OF THE ZODIAC

Diameter 11 in. This table was carved from a single piece of white jade. Carved into it are the twelve animals of the Chinese zodiac. It is in the shape of a flower, and carved at the base of each petal is either the symbol of infinity or the head of the mushroom of eternity.

161

WRITING SET

Height 3-9 in. The twelve pieces that compose this writing set represent the animals of the Chinese zodiac and were carved from a single block of rock crystal. These objects of exquisite manufacture were used both for practical purposes and as ornaments.

SMALL LEAF-SHAPED INKSTAND

Width 5 in. This piece in jadeite is shaped like a tapering leaf. Carved in the upper surface is a reservoir shaped like the head of a scepter (ruyi) that acted as the inkwell. Aside from serving a practical purpose, this object was also decorative.

PAPER KNIFE AND MAGNIFYING GLASS IN JADE

Length of paper knife 8¼ in; length of magnifying glass 9¼ in. Both objects have bare lines and are in green jade, although of very different tones. The handle of the magnifying glass is decorated with a carving of a dragon.

163

INKSTANDS IN JADEITE

164 *Width 4-7½ in. The piece in the foreground is decorated with leaves and a dragonfly in amber-color stone; the inkstand in the background, carved of green-streaked jadeite, bears plant motifs and rests on feet in the shape of turtles.*

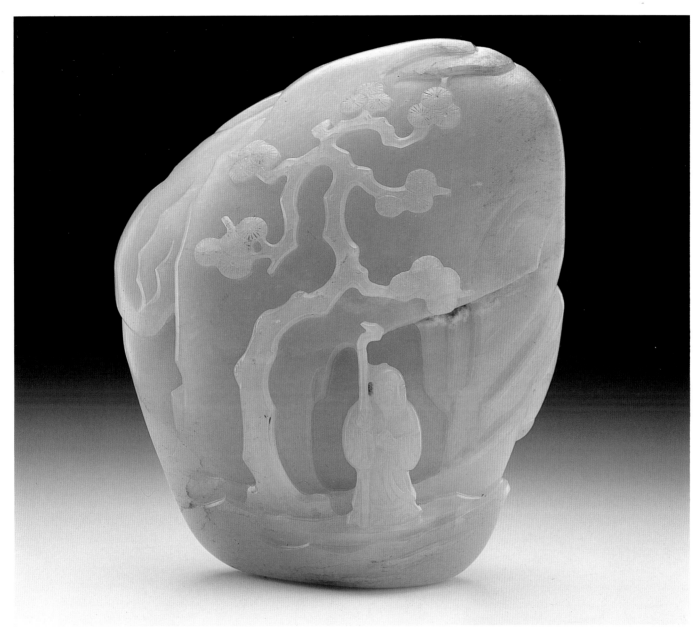

SHAN-TZU *IN SAPPHIRE*

*Height 4 ¼ in. This shan-tzu, an ornamental
piece in precious stone purposely shaped to
look like a rock, bears a simple relief carving
of a hermit at the feet of a tree. Another
human figure appears on the back, as seen in
the illustration at right.*

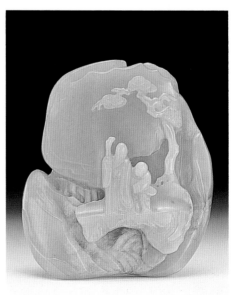

SHAN-TZU *WITH LANDSCAPE*

Following pages (166-67): *Length 12 ½ in. This piece was well
carved from a single block of white jade. Visible are a
mountain, small pagodas, walls, and trees. The engraved
ideograms are a poem written by an emperor.*

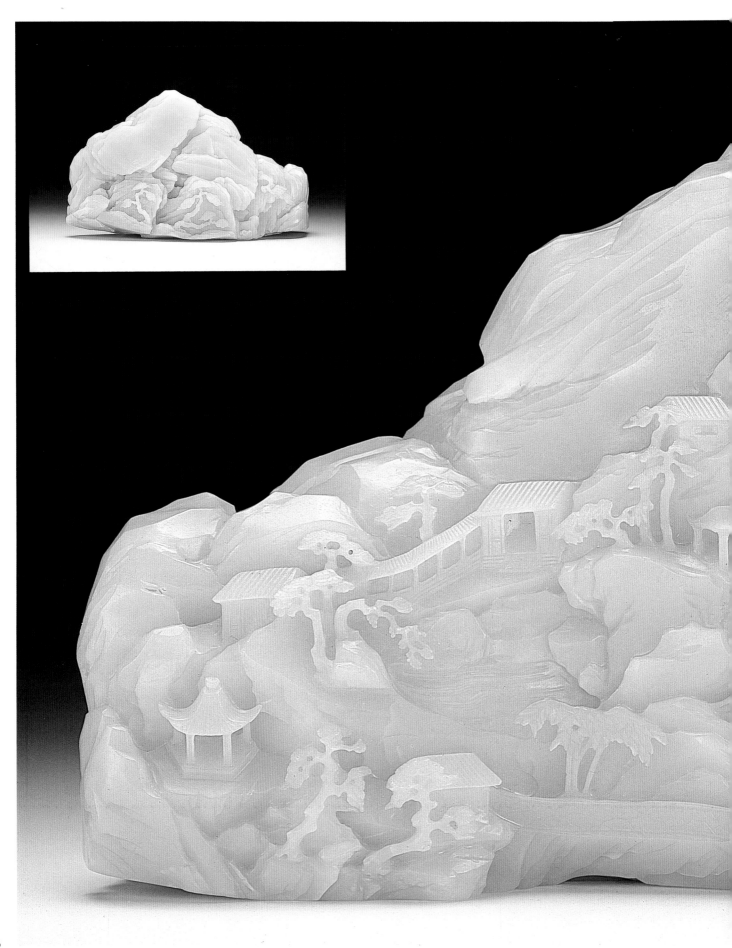

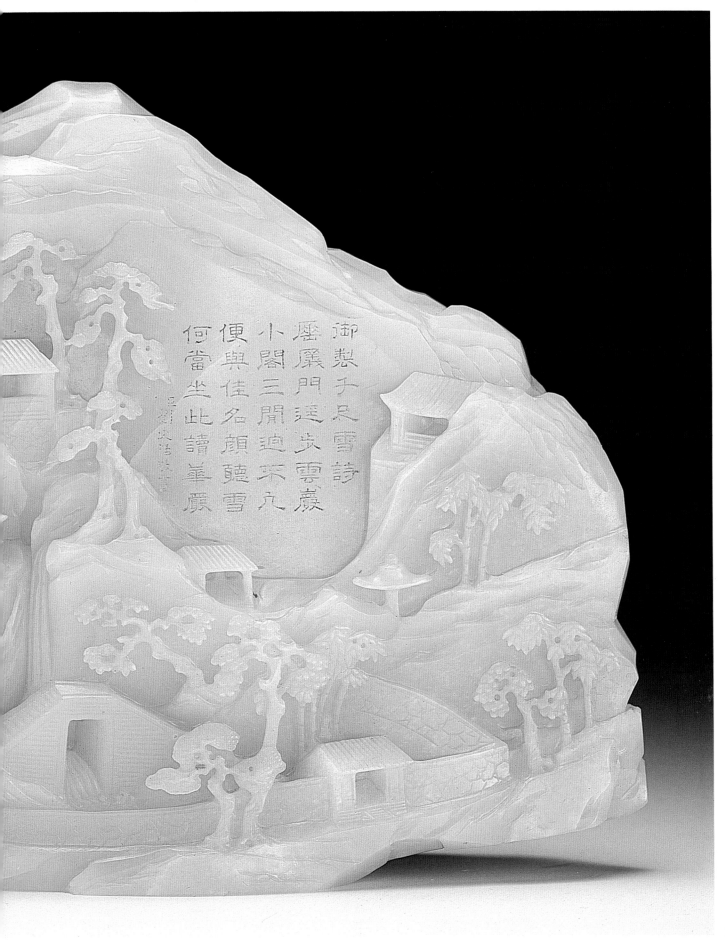

御製千尺雪詩
歷屐門逕尖雲巖
小閣三間迎眾凡
便與佳名顏䗹雪
何當坐此讀峰巒

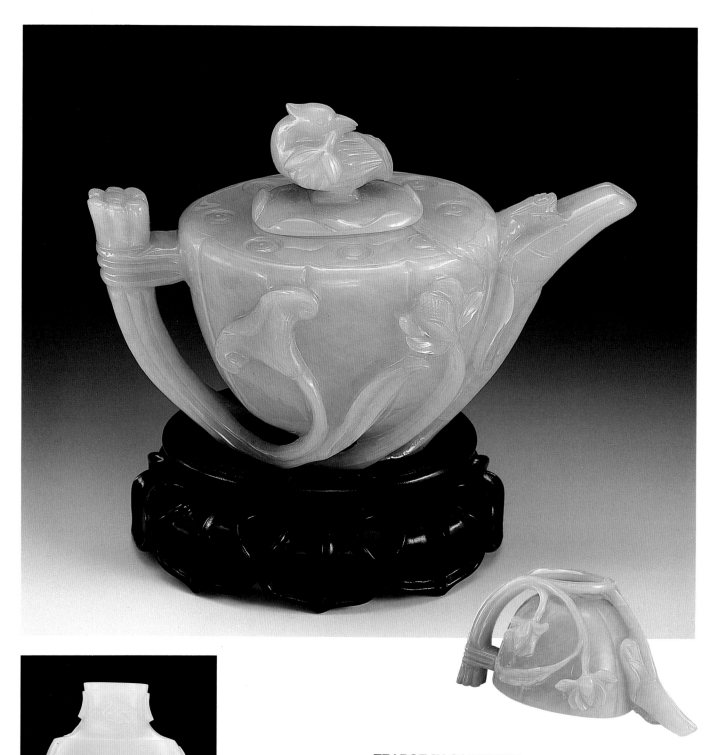

TEAPOT IN SAPPHIRE

Length 6 in; height 4 in. A bird with a flower in its beak acts as knob for the small cover. Around the body spreads a decorative theme of lotus roots that form the side handle. Mushrooms of eternity are carved in relief on the opposite side.

VASE IN WHITE JADE

Height 6½ in. From the narrow, undecorated mouth the body expands with relief carvings of various fanciful decorations, including the figure of a crane. The cover has been lost.

168

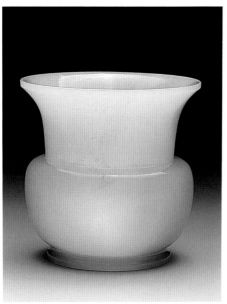

TEAPOT IN WHITE JADE

Height 5½ in. This piece was carved from stone of incomparable quality. The central band and spout are decorated with the "tao-tie" motif. Decorations of clouds are carved into the handle, and the knob of the cover is in the shape of a flower.

SAIL BOAT IN JADEITE

Following pages (170-71): *Height 6½ in. This piece represents a fishing boat. Four fishermen in various poses can be seen busy at work. A chain is attached to the boat's prow.*

TSA-DOU *IN WHITE JADE*

Left: *Diameter 3⅓ in; height 3¼ in. The tsa-dou is a table container made to hold leftovers. The example shown here is of very fine quality white jade. The neck and outer band are undecorated. This was used only by the royal family.*

BOWL IN WHITE JADE

*Width 10 in. This piece is of white jade from Hetian. The
handles are shaped like bats and have supporting arms
underneath. The interior surface is decorated in relief with
two pieces of fruit, flowers, steles, and leaves. These are
symbolic figures of longevity and happiness.*

172

BOWL IN WHITE JADE

Diameter 5 in. This piece was made of jade of excellent quality. The lip of the mouth is flared, and the body rests on a ring base. Two thin double bands are carved in relief all around the external surface, beneath the lip. Four ideograms written inside the base relate that the piece was "made during the reign of Jia Qing" (1796-1820).

BOWL IN WHITE JADE

Diameter 5 in; height 2 in. Made of high-quality material, this piece is without decoration and has a bare and elegant line. The bottom of the internal surface bears an inscription that reads "made during the reign of Jia Qing" (1796-1820). This piece was used by the royal family.

173

BASIN IN JADEITE

Diameter 6 in; height 2 in. This piece in green stone bears the image of a dragon sculpted with great mastery on the bottom of the external surface (below left).

BOWL IN TOPAZ

Height 5¼ in; diameter 3¾ in. This object is of particular value because of the stupendous, shiny stone from which it is carved. The body, which rests on a simple ring base, is without ornamental carvings, but a streak of slightly darker color seems to form a mountain landscape wrapped in mist.

PAIR OF CANDLESTANDS IN JADEITE

Diameter 4 in. Each of these two pieces is decorated with the figures of five bats and a Zhou character that symbolize happiness and longevity.

BOX IN JASPER

Length 4 in; width 2½ in. The cover of this piece bears low-relief carving of grass and leaf motifs. Although used for practical purposes, this box was also a decorative object.

BANANA-LEAF INKSTAND

Length 5 ¼ in. This object is made of agate and shows great skill. A ring is inserted in the stalk of the leaf as a further ornamental element.

INKSTAND IN AGATE

Length 4 ¼ in. This object bears animal and plant motifs symbolic of good luck.

INKSTAND WITH SHELLS

Length 3 ½ in. This piece in agate is delicately carved with marine motifs.

PAIR OF BOWLS WITH COVERS

Height 2¾ in; diameter 5½ in. These two pieces are made of white jade in the style of Hindustan. Ornamental motifs are carved on both the cover and the body, which elegantly stands on a ring base that reflects the handle on the cover.

FLOWER VASE IN AGATE

Width 6¼ in. This piece is made in agate in imitation of a bamboo brush holder. It is decorated with motifs of pines and mushrooms of longevity.

BRUSH HOLDER IN ROCK CRYSTAL

Height 6¼ in. This piece is made in imitation of a bamboo brush holder. Cranes are carved in high relief.

SPHERE OF ROCK CRYSTAL

Opposite: Diameter 4¼ in. Working with rock crystal is very difficult because it is an extremely hard stone. This sphere was made from material of matchless quality and rests on a base decorated with plant motifs.

INKSTAND IN ROCK CRYSTAL

Width 3 in. This piece was made of transparent, colorless, and excellent-quality rock crystal. It is in the form of a small bowl. Two dragons are carved in relief at the sides of the mouth.

179

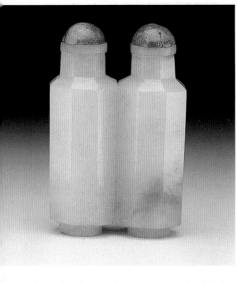

BOTTLES

Height 2-3 in. The bottles that appear on these and the next four pages were carved from various semiprecious stones, including jadeite, white jade, rock crystal, amber, and agate. Some are without decoration, others bear low-relief carvings, usually of symbols of happiness, longevity, or spring.

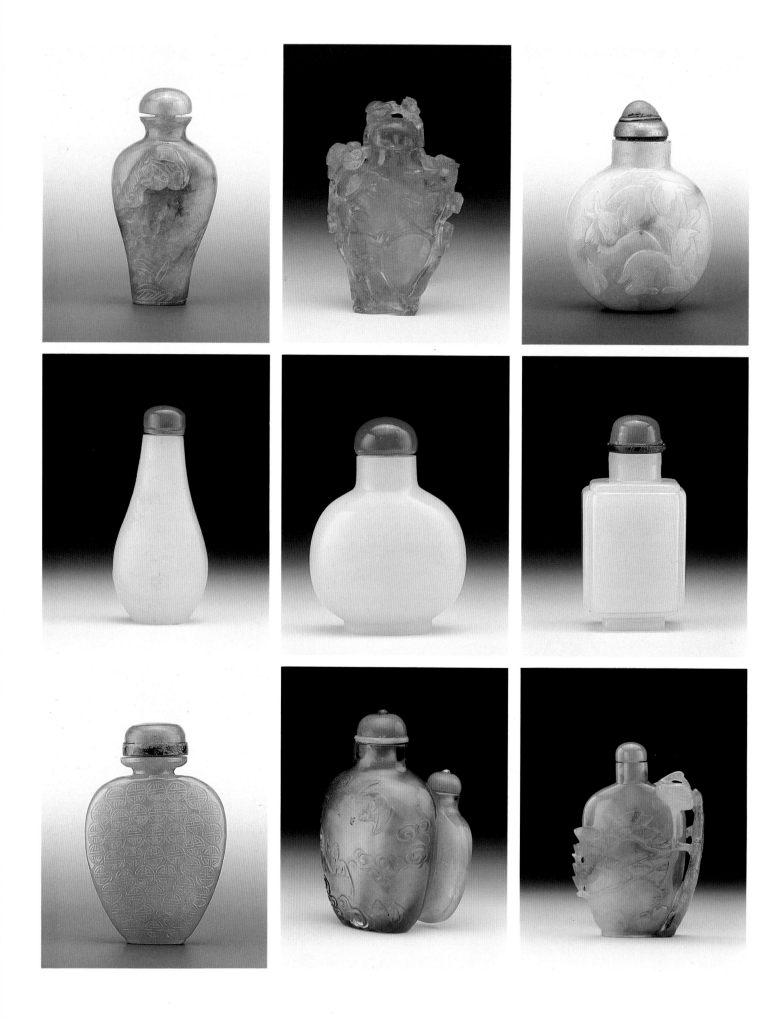

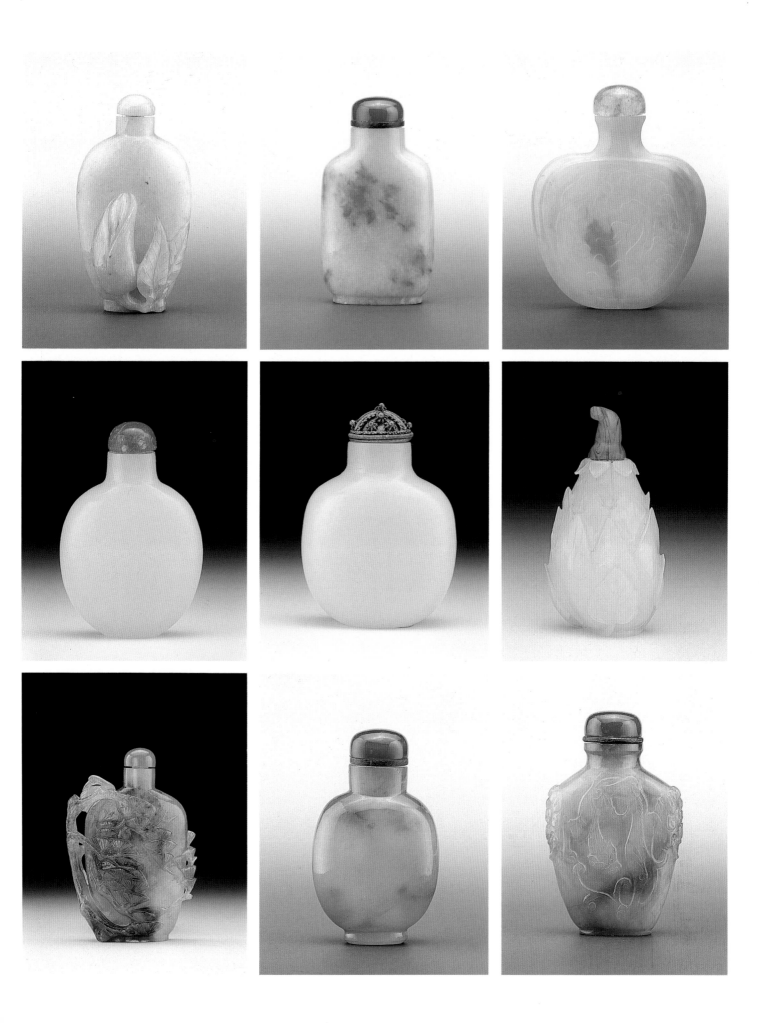

Jade accessories

During the reign of the Manchurian dynasty of Qing, the ruling class, which obviously belonged to the Manchurian race, faced the problem of how to behave in terms of Chinese tradition. In other words, the members of that class faced the question of whether to adapt to Chinese fashions and customs or instead rigidly preserve their own racial identity, their differences, and thus emphasize in that sense the distance between the ruling class and the subject people. In the end the Manchurians adopted Confucian customs and traditions while preserving, as far as possible, their own customs and traditions. Thus, the fashion of the Qing period mirrors a double-track line: with the consequence not only that clothes, garments in the strict sense, were sometimes Manchurian and sometimes "Han," but accessories for dress and clothing followed the same route and, as was foreseeable, led to a variety of accessories more vast and rich than had ever been seen in China.

No distinction can be made between accessories made for men and those used only by women; the use of these accessories was promiscuous. There were accessories for covering the head and the hair, and during the Manchurian period the characteristic dress for the hair was the long tail that falls onto a man's shoulders. This famous pigtail was created by growing the hair of the nape of the neck, while shaving the hair of the temples. This was an ancient Manchurian style, imposed on the Chinese beginning during the 17th century and abolished only with the coming of the republic (1912). To this style are related hair clips made like large rings (of jade for the well-to-do) suitable for holding the hair behind the neck; these were used only by men. For women the clips were instead long pins that were inserted in the mass of hair to hold it in place. Also used were forks and combs with large teeth. Such accessories were often made of jade. Also sometimes made of jade were the pins used to hold down headdresses and the pendants that often appeared on headdresses.

Moving down the body, immediately under the head is the neck, which the women adorned with one or more necklaces. The necklace is a typically female article of jewelry, which women wear to increase their beauty and to indicate their social rank. But there was also a type of necklace worn by men, by high dignitaries, required on certain official ceremonial occasions: it was widespread during the Qing period and most of all during the reign of Qian Long and consisted of a small cord on which were strung 108 jade beads. The number of jade beads was certainly functional in a magical sense, in which it was calculated that 108 is the result of multiples of 3, or 3 to the fourth plus 3 to the third. The numbers 3 and 9 were full of mysterious meaning: for example, according to tradition, Lao-tse wrote a book made up of 81 chapters (thus, 3 to the fourth) and, again according to tradition, was born "old" (Lao), being 81 years old at the moment he was born. Thus the high functionary protected himself by using the correct magical numbers. Chinese clothes did not have buttons in the sense of buttons on Western clothes, but there were clasps, called buttons because of the function they carried out, that of holding closed an article of clothing. Such buttons can be very elaborate, carved like small but precious works of art, and were most often made of jade (others were of ivory or wood). Even the buckles for holding belts were often masterpieces of jade, carved with precision, often in the form of small scepters: such accessories were often made of white jade and, as a variant, of sapphire. These works drew their inspiration from animals and fruits because in that way, aside from providing room for the most imaginative and refined artistic creations, they bore in themselves symbolic meanings, of good luck, health, or riches.

The wardrobe of the Chinese dignitary, whether Manchurian or not, also included shoe and glove clasps, small jade accessories made of a hook and clasp used to close either gloves at the wrist or hold closed cloth shoes. It would be useless to speak of rings made for women, since the variety of objects in that field is far too vast; and the same would apply to bracelets, because they vary according to the precious stone, including jade, and include cloisonné with settings in precious stones. Often encountered in the bracelet is the presentation of the serpent biting its own tail. It should be noted that even men, at least those of the high society, wore jade rings, usually on the thumb. Another object, always made of jade, that was part of the wardrobe of dignitaries or at least of well-to-do men, was the snuff box, those wonderful knickknacks collected today by many Westerners.

By way of these objects the Chinese reveal their high level of refinement and show themselves to have taste and to be the heirs of a great tradition. It is thus true that the Manchurians, as foreign as they were to the Chinese tradition, were fascinated by it and became subject to it.

HAIR PINS IN JADE

Following pages (190-91): Length 3½-6 in. These are various models of hair pins used by noblewomen of the Qing period to embellish their hairstyles. The upper part of these objects is often decorated with fantasy carvings of exquisite workmanship.

ACCESSORIES IN PRECIOUS STONE

Length 1-4 in. Small utilitarian objects like buckles and clasps (below and opposite) were often made in jade and other precious stones. Refined carving contributes to making these wonderfully ornamental.

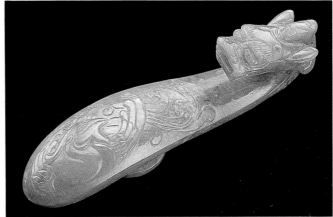

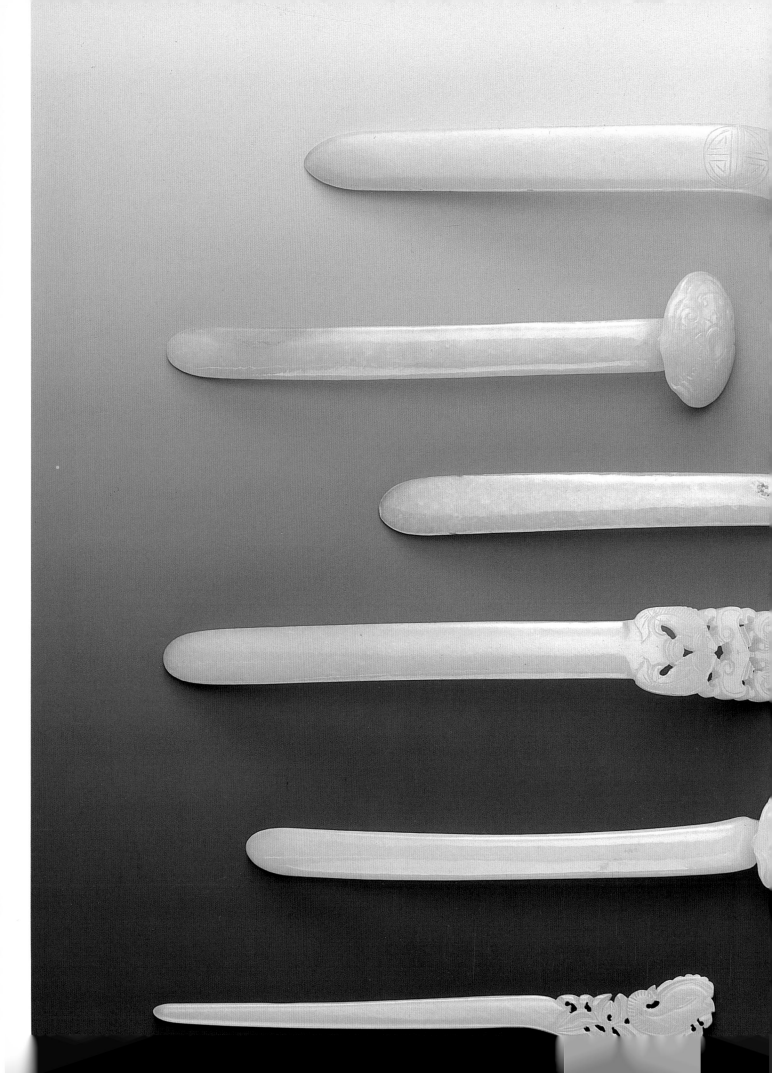

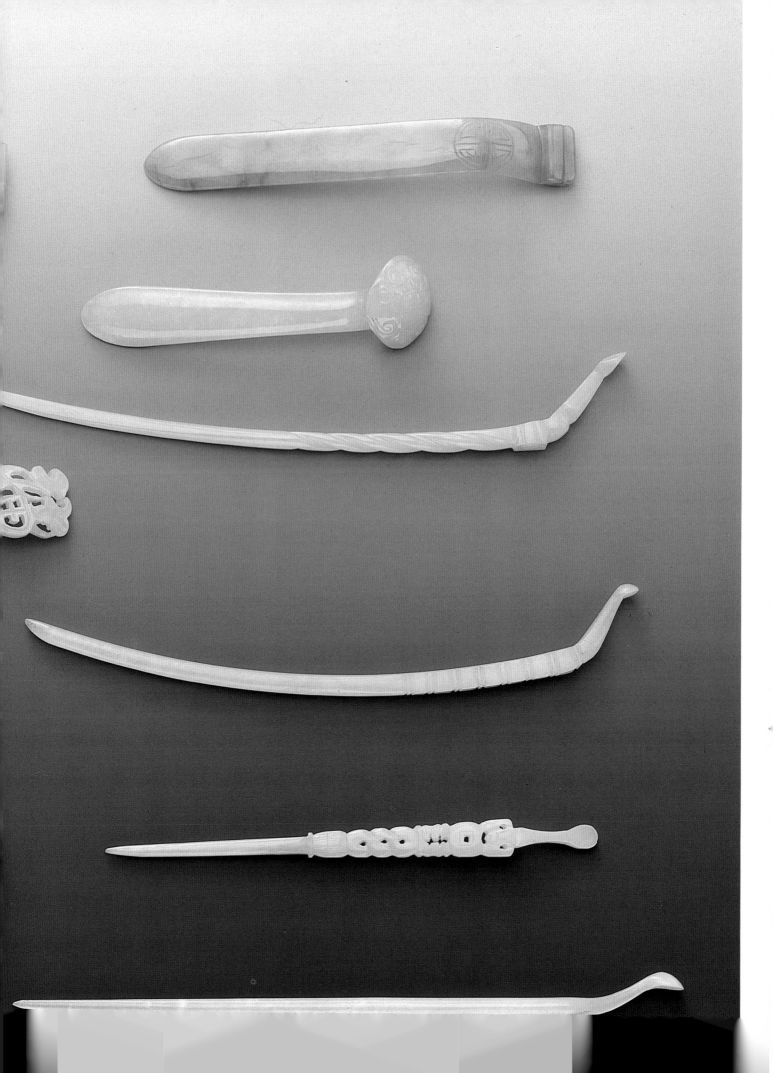

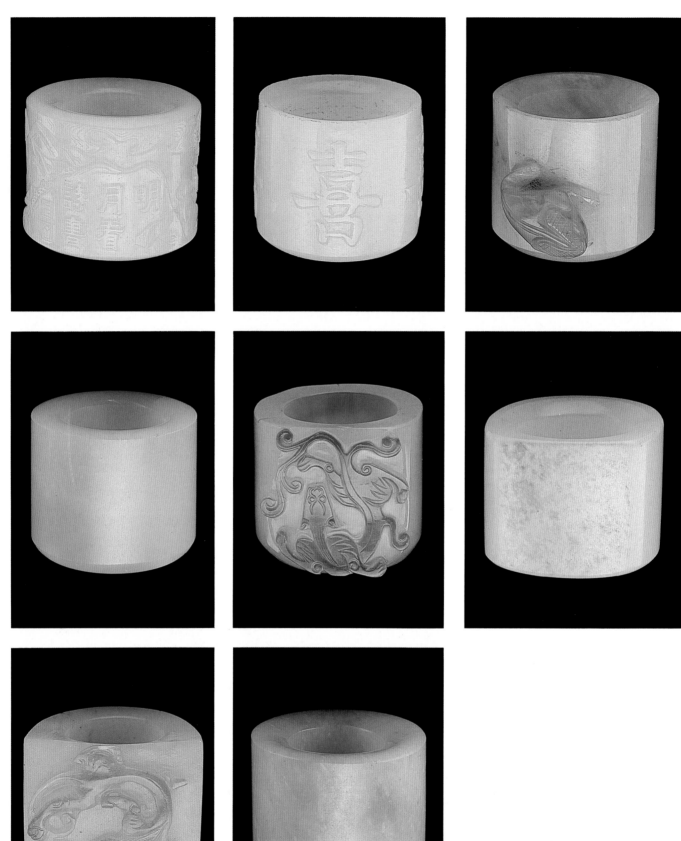

THUMB RINGS

Diameter ¾-1 in. These rings, originally used in drawing bows, later became purely ornamental objects. During the Qing period they were made in jade and were made both without decoration and with imaginative carvings.

THUMB RINGS IN JADEITE

Diameter 1 ¼ in. The ring to the left is in white jadeite decorated with a relief with symbolic motifs in amber color; the example to the right is worked smooth in streaked green stone.

SMALL ACCESSORIES IN JADEITE

*Length 1½-3 in. The small ornaments that appear on this
page were made in stone of excellent quality and bear
skillfully executed decorations.*

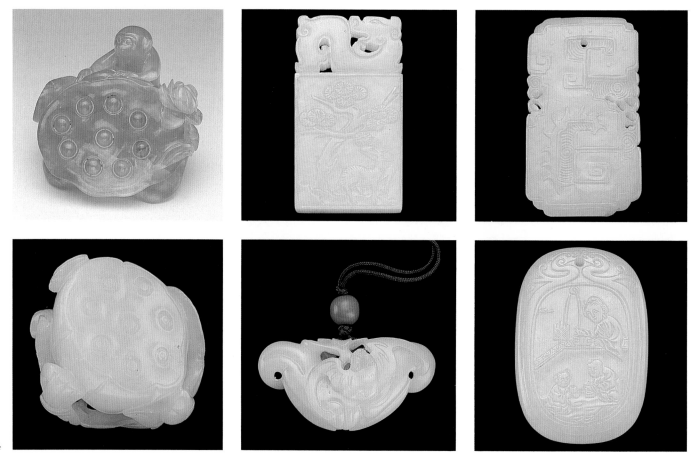

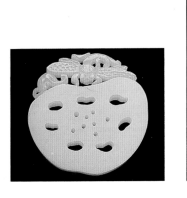

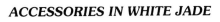

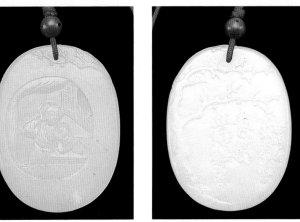

ACCESSORIES IN WHITE JADE

Height 2½-3¼ in; width 2-2¼ in. The buckles and pendants illustrated on this page are in different styles and bear various kinds of carving (from human figures to abstract signs), but all bear good luck symbols.

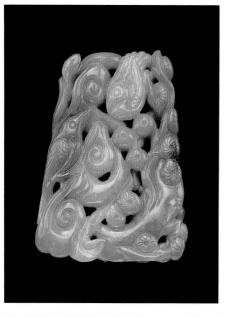

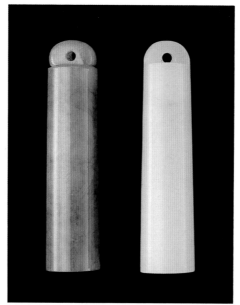

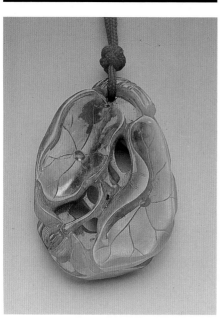

ACCESSORIES IN JADEITE

Length 1½-3 in. All these pieces are made in stone of superior quality with various colorations; the forms and decorations bear witness to exceptional artistic talents.

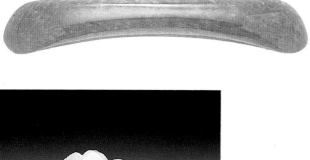

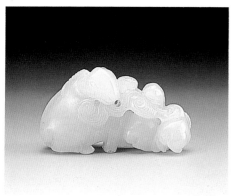

196

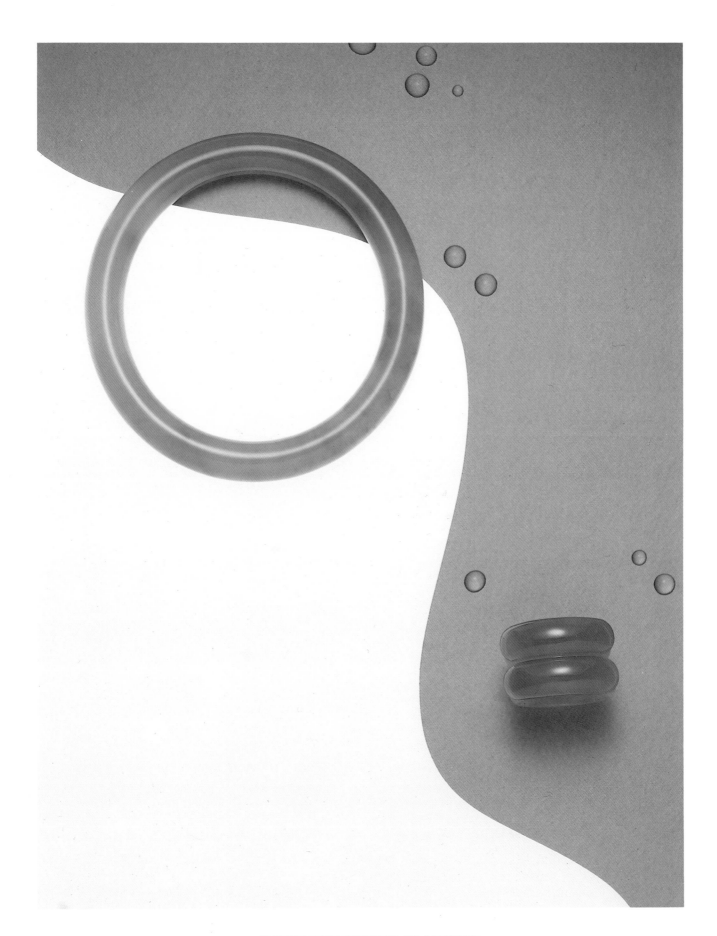

SADDLE TRAPPINGS IN JADEITE

The pieces of green jadeite illustrated here are splendid for their bare simplicity.   197

New jewels

The use of jade in today's ornamental arts is partly related to the revived interest in ethnographic jewels, but it is also a reflection of a deep longing to recover in the present the lost significance of ancient decorative rites in which the aesthetic function of jewelry represented only one aspect, and that often marginal, of its rich semantic vocabulary.

A symbol of power and social distinction, an allusive metaphor of mystical and religious values, jewelry has always been eloquent, a specific indication of the person who wears it; and in the case of jade, it revealed precise esoteric and romantic messages, for it was tied to ideas of immortality, incorruptibility, and protection against the perils of life and the dangers of death. During our age, with the enormous growth of the jewelry industry and the consequent mass production of jewelry in series, jewelry has inexorably entered the world of standardization, thus losing much of its original symbolic value and often being reduced to mere ornament—if not, in fact, being no more than a display of wealth. This is not the case with jade, however, for the delicate shades of its crystals still preserve a wide spectrum of evocations and the secret ciphers of a talismanic magic. These characteristics, together with jade's intrinsic value and its increasing scarcity, have made it a material much sought by master jewelers throughout the world. As with all other types of jewelry, the composition of jade jewelry mirrors the customs, design, stylistic peculiarities, and characteristic themes of the periods in which it is made and expresses the spirit and the inclinations, sometimes overlapping and contradictory, of the dominant fashion.

Our own century has witnessed a singular eclecticism in jade jewelry that has wound from decade to decade along various threads and different typologies. Because of its physical characteristics and surprising shades, this wonderful gift from nature lends itself in particular to combinations with precious metals as well as with coral, pearls, amber, and many other colored stones, and thus jade has won a permanent place in the repertoire of so-called classic jewelry, always offering new decorative creations and eternal elegance. In the form of drops, boules, pendants, cabochons, splendid amulet sculptures, and refined cameos, jade, in its rarest varieties, such as emerald green jadeite, the preferred stone of the emperors of ancient China, has marked in different but always refined ways the important stages of 20th-century jewelry. During the Art Nouveau period it was worked in sinuous silhouettes inspired by floral or zoomorphic motifs; during the period of Art Deco it was put in rigorous geometric forms with pure lines. Since then, from one period to the next, drops and spheres of jade, with their charming shades that dissolve from white to green to blue, were all the rage in the shining *animalier* brooches and the flowers, boxes, and bouquets created by the great jewelers of the 1940s and 1950s, in splendid company with glittering multicolor gems, evocative of treasures closed in the tombs of sultans or maharajas. Aside from pins, jade became an accomplice and a protagonist of other elegant ornaments, on royal diadems and sometimes on gold or platinum mountings with pearls, rubies, sapphires, emeralds, and diamonds. From distant regions of the Orient, from the generous mines of Burma, passing through the hands of expert gem cutters, it became the dominant motif of sumptuous necklaces that, matched with gold and gems, emphasized the quality and the secret fascination of the rarest jadeite. The vast range of jewelry made in jade also includes rings, which call to mind the ancient rings worn by women and men in imperial China to indicate their position among the highest castes, those of the dignitaries, functionaries, and members of court. Sometimes we find true masterpieces of the art of stone cutting, with seals and cameos of the finest forms held in mountings of precious metals. The variety of contemporary production also includes rich necklaces, with one or more strands, composed of beads of various sizes, often carved or engraved with motifs taken from ancient Oriental iconography. Such motifs are revived and reworked on the polished surfaces of various bracelets and on the pendants that fall like amulets from chains and necklaces, creating cultural and ethnographic evocations that add a touch of personality and a sense of magic to the jewelry. Thus is renewed that invisible thread that ties contemporary jade jewelry to the earliest Chinese ornamental art and to the complex symbolism expressed by that art. On the threshold of the year 2000, both the largest production houses and the smallest artisan workshops have found that the expressive potentialities of the "imperial stone" make it an invaluable ally for their creations. It is an ally that, in the name of a glorious past and a brilliant future, rises above and goes beyond any style, any current or trend, to become a timeless classic.

199

200   *Necklace in jadeite with diamond-studded clasp.*

Double-strand necklace in jadeite alternating with circular disks in yellow gold and diamonds.

Hexagonal earrings in jadeite framed
by an edge of diamonds.

202 Artistic ring of *animalier inspiration with cabochon in
jadeite illuminated by small diamonds.*

Pin with central body in carved jadeite
enclosed by a double crown of diamonds.

*Earrings in jadeite and diamonds
with three-link pendants.*

204   *Leaf-shape earrings with pendants in finely worked jadeite.*

*Chain in yellow gold with cylindrical pendant in jadeite
with ends in gold inlaid with diamonds.*

*Art Deco bracelet with circular motifs
in jadeite alternating with disks that
enclose symbolic subjects in diamonds.*

206

Art Deco pins of naturalistic inspiration in gold, platinum, jadeite, diamonds, pearls, and rubies.

Precious necklace composed of grains of
jadeite, Maltese cross motifs, and central
208 diamond-studded floral design.

*Original-style necklace in jadeite
worked in fantasy* animalier *motifs
interspersed with diamonds of
various cut.*

209

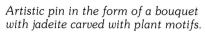

Artistic pin in the form of a bouquet with jadeite carved with plant motifs.

Left: *Pin in the shape of a dragonfly with wings in delicate filigree and body in jadeite broken by bands of diamonds.* Below: *Large ring with central jadeite piece framed by diamonds.*

Pin composed of a cluster of granules of jadeite illuminated by vine-shoots of diamonds.

Ring with large cabochon in jadeite embellished by diamonds arranged as a corolla.

211

Earrings in pure jadeite in semicircles with
carvings and as intertwined rings.

Circle bracelet in jadeite and circle bracelet in jade carved with fantasy motifs.

Double-strand of cultivated pearls with Art Deco clasp in
214 jadeite in an interwoven motif bordered by diamonds.